The Wisdom of Alfred Edersheim

The Wisdom of Alfred Edersheim

Gleanings from a 19th Century Jewish Christian Scholar

DAVID MISHKIN

WIPF & STOCK · Eugene, Oregon

THE WISDOM OF ALFRED EDERSHEIM
Gleanings from a 19th Century Jewish Christian Scholar

Copyright © 2008 David Mishkin. All rights reserved. Except for brief quotations in critical publications or reviews, no part of this book may be reproduced in any manner without prior written permission from the publisher. Write: Permissions, Wipf and Stock Publishers, 199 W. 8th Ave., Suite 3, Eugene, OR 97401.

Wipf & Stock
A Division of Wipf and Stock Publishers
199 W. 8th Ave., Suite 3
Eugene, OR 97401

www.wipfandstock.com

ISBN 13: 978-1-55635-939-2

Dedicated to Norm Fuller – Pastor, friend, man of God and all-around good guy who helped make this book possible.

Contents

Introduction ix

His Life 1

His Bibliography 8

His Legacy 17

His Magnum Opus 22

His Quotes 25

APPENDIX A: *Whose is Thine Heart?* 175

APPENDIX B: *From Grey to Dawn* 187

APPENDIX C: The Athenaeum 193

APPENDIX D: Eulogy from a Fellow Oxford Professor 196

Introduction

I FIRST DISCOVERED ALFRED Edersheim about twenty years ago. I was taking a 'Life of Christ' course and one of the required texts was *The Life and Times of Jesus the Messiah*. As a Jew who was a new believer in Jesus, I was amazed and delighted. I devoured it. Here was another Jewish believer from a century earlier – a professor from Oxford, no less – who was considered the leading authority on Jewish history and customs in the early Christian era! And in the midst of his scholarly discussions, he wrote in the most descriptive, imaginative and passionate way. He was a scholar with a pastor's (and a poet's) heart.

The Life and Times of Jesus the Messiah is an unparalleled commentary on the Gospels. Spanning over 1,000 pages, Edersheim's interaction with history and scripture abounds with references from ancient sources. He was thoroughly acquainted with the works of Philo, Josephus, Rabbinic and Apocryphal literature, and the Greek and Roman writings of the Classical period. They all seem second nature to him in their original languages. His scholarship remains remarkably relevant today, even though a number of archaeological finds in the last century have altered the playing field of this area of study. The Dead Sea Scrolls, for example, were not even discovered until 58 years after his death.

More recently, some of Edersheim's other books have become of interest in Christian circles. There is now more of a desire among believers – both Jewish and Gentile alike – to study the Jewish roots of our Christian faith. And Edersheim was uniquely qualified to teach us, having been an expert in both Jewish and Christian studies. He wrote many volumes in a variety of genres, including novels. Most of these books are extremely rare and hard to find. This is why, I believe, it is time for such a book as this. It is meant to be an encyclopedia as well as a celebration of his writings. There are similar collections from great men of faith by the likes of C.S. Lewis, Charles Spurgeon, Oswald Chambers and A.W. Tozer. The words of Alfred Edersheim are every bit as topical, interesting and

Introduction

inspiring. They will also help us in understanding his own life and times. Interestingly, he was somewhat skeptical about traditional biographies.

> *There is to observant minds a peculiar taint about many religious biographies. They may be exceedingly well meant, and very devoutly written. But, viewed as biographies, they are simply not true. The statement may seem startling; it is only too correct. Who has ever met such people in real life? And thankful we are that the answer will be in the negative; since otherwise no hope of being Christians would be left to us, not to any persons living outside printed books. For, assuredly, there is not a warp without a woof, nor light without shadow, nor yet a life without failings, foibles, and the thousand and one little things which give to character its individuality, and to life its peculiarity, but which are carefully left out of so many biographies.*[1]

In fact, he was specifically asked by his children to write his biography. They thought it would be quite interesting to many people. In response he quipped:

> *No. I have played the dancing-bear long enough in my life before the eyes of people, to wish to do it when I am dead.*[2]

It will be helpful for the reader to keep in mind the time and place of his writings. The language used is very much that of Victorian England, and specifically consistent with religious writings of the period. By today's standards he can seem pietistic or overly dramatic. And remember, English was not his first language, nor even his second or third. He did not even begin to learn English until he was studying medicine at the University of Budapest. His tone, especially when dealing with Jesus' relationship with the Synagogue (and rabbinic law in general), can appear too polemical in some of his writings. But this too must be taken in its context.

> *None loved Israel so intensely, even unto death, as Jesus of Nazareth; none made such withering denunciations as He of Jewish Traditionalism, in all its branches, and of its Representatives. It is with Traditionalism, not the Jews, that our controversy lies.*[3]

The quotes below are arranged alphabetically by category, with some longer portions in the appendices. The quotes mostly fall into one of

---

1. Elisha, 174
2. Tohu, 141
3. LTJM, xviii

Introduction

several camps. Many are devotional comments, bringing to light lessons of faith and practice for followers of Jesus. He seems to have a special fondness for the providence of God, the Kingdom of God, and issues of growth and service for believers. However, he is probably best known for his biblical and theological commentaries. Many of the quotes offer insight to various aspects of Biblical history, Jewish studies and scholarly research. Another area which interested Edersheim was apologetics; defending and proclaiming the faith in response to critical scholarship. Finally, many of the quotes relate to the Jewish / Christian debate, and have value for understanding the Jewish background of the respective topics. These include views about messianic prophecies, the teachings of the rabbis, and the issue of atonement.

His Life

THERE IS RELATIVELY LITTLE written about the life of Alfred Edersheim. The best source of information comes from *Tohu-Va-Vohu*, a collection of his writings which was published a year after his death. His daughter, Ella, compiled some of his unpublished thoughts and added some basic facts about his life. All other attempts to recreate his biography have borrowed heavily from this. Another good source is the memoir of Edersheim's contemporary, Adolph Saphir. Several dictionaries and encyclopedias[1] also provide an entry for him, but usually include the same brief information from the above sources. There are several books which chronicle the lives of Jewish believers in Jesus,[2] but here too the information on him is limited. The study of missions history, especially the Scottish Mission to the Jews (see below), has been helpful to the discussion. And in the early 1990s, there were two important studies written about Edersheim. One was an article which appeared in the Michigan Theological Journal[3] and the other was a paper given at a missions conference.[4]

The Rev. Dr Alfred Edersheim was born into a Jewish home in Vienna on March 7, 1825, the youngest of four children. His father, Marcus, was

---

1. For example: *The Oxford Dictionary of the Christian Church*, (Oxford University Press, 1997), p. 530; *The New Schaff-Herzog Encyclopedia of Religious Knowledge* (NY, Baker, 1958), p. 75; *The New International Dictionary of the Christian Church* (Grand Rapids, Zondervan, 1979), p. 328, *Dictionary of Scottish Church History and Theology* (Downers Grove, Intervarsity Press, 1993), p. 275

2. Gartenhaus, Jacob, *Famous Hebrew Christians* (Grand Rapids, Baker Book House, 1979); Meyers, Louis, *Eminent Hebrew Christians of the 19th Century* (NY, Edwin Mellon Press, 1983 – originally published in 1913); Bernstein, Aaron, *Some Jewish Witnesses for Christ* (Operative Jewish Convert's Institute, 1909), Einspruch, Henry, *Jewish Confessors of the Faith* (Baltimore, Jewish Missions Committee, United Lutheran Church of America, 1925)

3. Mayhew, Eugene, J., "Alfred Edersheim: A Brief Biography," MJT 22, 1991

4. Bond, Lynn Rosen, "The Life and Times of Alfred Edersheim," February 28, 1991, Lausanne Consultation on Jewish Evangelism

a banker from Holland. His mother, Stephanie Beifuss Edersheim, was from Frankfurt, Germany.[5]

Adolph Saphir wrote the following:

> He had been brought up luxuriously in Vienna, and was one of the leaders in fashion. He was highly educated, spoke Latin fluently, knew Greek, German, French, Hebrew, Hungarian and Italian. When [Adolph] Cremieux, head of the French Bar and in 1848 French Minister of Justice, visited Vienna he was welcomed by an address given by Edersheim on behalf of Jewish youth. The address was given when Cremieux attended the synagogue, and Edersheim had been chosen as the young peoples' representative. Cremieux was so impressed by the young Edersheim's oratory that he desired to take him to Paris under his patronage and provision for life, to train him as a barrister. Edersheim's family, however, would not allow him to go.[6]

In 1841 Edersheim entered the University of Vienna to study philosophy and medicine. There he became one of the founders of the democratic club, and was active in public discussions and debates. Suddenly, his father lost his wealth, and Edersheim transferred to Pest (Budapest) to continue his education. This move would prove to be quite providential in regard to his faith. In Pest he earned money as a tutor of various languages. He again involved himself in "the liberal element" and was considered "dangerous" by the censors because of some of the topics of his writings.[7] Pest also had a thriving Jewish community, which had recently been undergoing some changes.

> At the genesis of the Pest Jewish community, it was orthodox in its outlook, but the leaders were enlightened and receptive of the changes that Moses Mendelssohn promoted. Due to demands of the reform-minded Jewish elite, there was a disruption in the Jewish community after the death of Rabbi Israel Wallman in 1826 ... The decisive year for the Pest Jewish community was 1833 when the election of a new rabbi emerged as an issue. In 1836, after long and careful considerations rabbi Low Schwab was chosen to be the rabbi in Pest as a compromise between the Orthodox and the

---

5. Tohu, vii

6. Carlyle, Gavin, *Mighty in the Scriptures, A Memoir of Adolf Saphir* (London, J.F. Shaw and Co., 1893)

7. Meyers, 54

> Reform trends . . . During his time Pest became the leading political, religious and economic centre of Hungarian Jewry.[8]

Meanwhile, there had been much excitement in the Church of Scotland regarding Jewish evangelism, largely centering around the role of Israel in biblical eschatology. Leading figures in the movement included Robert M. McCheyne and Andrew Bonar. At a speech before the general assembly of the Free Church of Scotland, Bonar declared: 'when we give the Jews their proper place in our missionary work, we might look for special blessing at home, for, "Blessed is he who blesseth thee."[9]

The Scottish Mission first sent a delegation to Palestine to consider missionary possibilities. On route in Egypt, one from among the delegation fell off his camel. This, in turn, led to events which required them to pass through Pest on their return trip. In Pest they would meet the Archduchess Maria Dorothea (the wife of Archduke Joseph – the uncle of the Austrian Emperor). Dorothea was a devout woman who had been praying for seven years that God would send people to carry the gospel to that city. She would prove to be an important ally for the Church of Scotland's work in that part of the world. In 1841, John Duncan became the first Scottish missionary to Pest.[10]

Edersheim began to study English as a student at Pest. His private tutor was a Jewish man named Dr. Pogros. When Pogros had to leave, he introduced Edersheim to Rev William Wingate, one of the missionaries from Scotland. Wingate was a former Glasgow merchant who loved the Jewish people. He had "a university education and some knowledge of theology."[11] This was another extraordinary turn of events.

> The Church historian, Ferenc Balogh remarked that this was a highly unusual event leaving a young Jew under the care of

---

8. Kovacs, Abraham, *The History of the Free Church of Scotland's Mission to the Jews in Budapest and it's Impact on the Reform Church of Hungary* (Frankfurt, Peter Lang, 2006), p. 22

9. Cited in Kovacs, p. 49

10. Dunlop, John, *Memories of Gospel Triumphs Among the Jews During the Victorian Era* (London, S.W. Partridge, 1894), p. 13 also: McDougal, David, *In Search of Israel, A Chronicle of the Jewish Missions of the Church of Scotland* (London, T. Nelson, 1941), p. 22–53

11. Kovacs, 74

Protestant missionaries. Balogh attributed it to the recognition of Duncan's influence and acceptance by the Jewish community.[12]

Wingate was the first to give Edersheim a New Testament, which made a profound impression on the young student. Jacob Gartenhaus, in his book *Famous Hebrew Christians*, recorded Edersheim's reaction to the gift.

> *From Wingate I received the New Testament. I shall never forget the impression Jesus' Sermon on the Mount made on me, nor the surprise and the profound feeling I experienced while reading the New Testament. The 'Christianity' which I knew as such hitherto was not Christianity. What I did not know was the teaching of Jesus which opened to me such unfathomable depths.*[13]

In those days, there were many Jews who underwent baptism as a means to furthering their political, social or economic situations, with no interest in the gospel itself. Therefore, special care was given to new Jewish believers to confirm their commitment. Edersheim (along with Adolph Saphir) began to study with John Duncan, whose great love for the Jewish people and his proficiency in Hebrew earned him the nickname "Rabbi" amongst his friends. Edersheim made a clear profession of faith and was baptized in April 1843. Almost immediately afterward, he began to teach English to other students, with the condition that the Bible would be the only lesson book.[14] Regarding some of these new Jewish believers he was teaching, Duncan wrote,

> In this city more than a hundred Hebrew converts have since been baptized in the name of "Him whom the nations abhor".... They used to read day after day the Epistles of Paul, as if they had been letters that had come by that morning's post.[15]

Another place where the Church of Scotland sent missionaries to the Jews was Iasi ("Jassy"), a city in the Northeastern part of Romania. The team was lead by Daniel Edward, who actually arrived in Hungary even before John Duncan arrived in Budapest. Edersheim joined Edward to reach his own people with the message of Jesus. There were consider-

---

12. ibid, p. 82
13. Gartenhaus, 76
14. Carlyle, 50
15. Stuart, A. Moody, *The Life of John Duncan* (Edinburgh, Banner of Truth Trust, 1991 – originally published in 1879), p. 71

able struggles, including organized opposition led by Rabbi Aaron Moses Ben Jacob Taubes of the ultra orthodox Chabad movement. There were also internal issues. According to records from the sending organization, Edersheim faced difficulties with the *Committee* over his intention to get married. There was also a disagreement between him and Daniel Edward regarding finances. Edersheim was cleared of all suspicion, but the *Committee* chose not to reinstate his services in Jassy.[16]

It was decided that Edersheim would return to Scotland with Duncan. At first, he had some difficulty leaving, as the government of Austria required all its citizens to serve in the military. Fortunately, a well known missionary to India (John Wilson) had just arrived in Budapest. He was regarded by authorities as a "man of distinction," and had considerable influence. He was allowed to take several people with him on his travels back to Scotland. Edersheim was chosen along with Saphir and one other, thus releasing them from military service.[17]

Edersheim went back to Scotland and joined Duncan to continue his studies. Duncan would become the first professor of Hebrew and Oriental languages at New College, Edinburgh. Edersheim later went to the University of Berlin to continue his theological education (studying under another noted Jewish believer in Jesus, August Neander). Although he was now 'off the mission field,' his identity as a Jew and his desire to reach his people with the gospel never wavered. His vast writings provide numerous examples of this. However, he apparently had reservations about some of the existing missionary structures.

> *Jew and Christian as I am, 'Missionary Meetings' are becoming odious to me. The benevolent pity over the poor Jew, by those who neither know nor can sympathise with him, my soul abhorreth.*[18]

In Scotland, Edersheim was ordained a Presbyterian minister. He served at Free College Church in Old Aberdeen and then relocated to Torquay. News of the scholar's arrival spread quickly, and he began to preach each week in a room in a hotel. As a result, The Scottish Church in Torquay was built specifically for him, and he became its first minister.[19]

---

16. Ross, John S., "Daniel Edward: Pioneer Missionary," Mishkan, Issue 47, 2006, p. 6
17. Carlyle, 48
18. Tohu, 107
19. Stephens, George, *Jewish Christian Leaders* (London, Oliphants, 1966), p. 38

He later joined the Church of England and became Vicar in Dorsetshire. Regarding his denominational affiliation, he said,

> I have passed from the Scotch to the English Church, and have not for one moment regretted the change. The changing was, and is, most unpleasant, but not the change; that has placed me where all my sympathies find most ample scope . . . I am convinced of the historical Church; I believe in a national Church; I prefer a liturgical Church – and on these grounds I have joined the Church of England.[20]

Alfred Edersheim married Mary Broomfield (a missionary from Scotland) in 1848. They had eight children: Stephanie Christina born December 16, 1848, Mary Matilda born October 5, 1851, Julia Augusta born November 12, 1854, Marcia Louisa born December 23, 1856, Alfred Edersheim Jr. born on October 17, 1858, Elise Williamina born May 12, 1860, Madeleine Anna born July 17, 1861 and Ella Georgina, who was christened on August 23, 1863.[21] They also had a dog – a Pomeranian – named Zing.[22] After Mary's death, which was some time between 1864 and 1869, Alfred married Sophia Hancock. His older brother Julius also became a follower of Jesus through his witness.[23] His daughter, Ella, collected his writings for the posthumously published *Tohu-Va-Vohu*. His other daughter, Elise Williamina, wrote several books of her own, including *The Laws and Polity of the Jews*,[24] *The Rites and Worship of the Jews*,[25] *A Lady Born* (novel),[26] *The School Mistress of Haven's End* (novel)[27] and *China Coast Tales*, under the pseudonym: Lise Boehm.[28] Also, in 1892 Francis Edersheim (relationship unknown, perhaps Julius's son?) wrote, *Israel in Chaldea, a Sacred Dramatic Cantata in One Part*.[29]

---

20. Tohu, 45
21. Mayhew, 182
22. Tohu, 141
23. Ibid, p. 20
24. Religious Tract Society, London, 1883
25. Religious Tract Society, London, 1890
26. Christian Knowledge Society, London, 1893
27. Religious Tract Society, London, 1900
28. Kelly and Walsh, Singapore, 1898
29. Edersheim, Francis, *Israel in Chaldea, A Sacred Dramatic Cantata in One Part*, (Hutchings and Romer, London, 1892)

His Life

One of the reasons for his various geographical moves concerned his health – he had been suffering with inflammation of the lungs. He also, according to Wingate, "was the only Hebrew Christian clergyman, so far as I know, who was invited by the late Dean Stanley to preach in Westminster Abbey, and by Dean Vaughan in the Temple Church." In 1882 he moved to Oxford and was appointed Grinfield Lecturer on the Septuagint at Oxford University. He taught and wrote there until 1889.[30] He went to France when his health deteriorated and soon afterwards died on March 16, 1889. He is buried in the cemetery of Mentone[31] and his theological and Judaica libraries were donated to Exeter College, Oxford. They are in a special collection[32] which (unfortunately) does not include any letters or other personal writings. As the final entry in *Tohu-Va-Vohu*, Ella Edersheim wrote,

> On a spur of the beautiful hill-side cemetery of Mentone he lies, looking straight towards Jerusalem, the city whose people he loved and tried to serve, and in whose spiritual counterpart he now beholds his King in all His beauty; and, having awaked up after His likeness, is satisfied with it.[33]

---

30. Carlyle, 51
31. Tohu, xxviii
32. Exeter College Library, shelf numbers: A.1 – I.12, PA 3.224, PC1.165 – PD 5.021
33. Tohu, xxviii

His Bibliography

THE FOLLOWING WORKS ARE the sources for the quotes which follow. The more popular books are quoted from updated editions so that readers may easily find them if they wish to examine their contexts. As more research is done, it is hoped that additional articles by Alfred Edersheim will be discovered.

1847, Jubilee Rhythm of St Bernard

J. Nisbet and Co., London. In this collection, Edersheim translated hymns and poems of St. Bernard (12th century) from the original Latin into English. There is no commentary on the material, only a brief explanation. He wrote, *"I have endeavored not only to be literal, but as much as possible to preserve the form of the original. This may perhaps, in part, be pled in excuse of harshness in the rendering. But I venture to lay it down a s a principle, that, while in translating prose writings, considerable latitude as to style and form may be allowed, often with very great advantage to the reader – in poetical writings, where so much depends on the form in which the thought is presented, on the words in which it is expressed, on the precise succession of lines, and occasionally even on the metre and the rhyme, every effort should be made to follow the original as closely as possible."* Edition cited: British Library shelf number: W91.5326.

1851, Whose is Thine Heart?

Partridge and Oakley, Paternoster Row. This was an address given at the *Foreign Conference and Evangelization Committee* in London. It is subtitled, *An Affectionate Address to Young People,* and it is based on Proverbs 23:26. The entire address appears here in Appendix A. Edition cited: British Library Shelf Number: 4406.b.82.(2)

His Bibliography

1856, History of the Jewish Nation from the Destruction of Jerusalem to the Establishment of Christianity in the Roman Empire

("Nation") T. and T. Clark Publishing. This book focuses on the important years after the destruction of the Temple in the year 70 AD. Topics include the origin of Talmudic Judaism, as well as Jewish interaction with both the Romans and the Jewish Christians of the day. Unlike some of his later works, the style is more factual, with fewer descriptive comments along the way. Still, it is extremely valuable for the student of this period of history. Chapters from this book which have also been published separately, include: *The Hebrew Commonwealth; The History of the Synagogue from the Destruction of Jerusalem to the Jewish War of Liberation; The Political and Religious State of the Jews After the Destruction of Jerusalem; The progress of Arts and Sciences Among the Hebrews*; Edition quoted: *The History of the Jewish Nation After the Destruction of Jerusalem Under Titus*, (Montana, Kessinger Publishing's Rare Reprints, 2004)

1856, Sketches of Jewish Social Life in the Days of Christ

("Sketches") This popular book covers everything from the geography, educational systems, family structures, trades, religious life and philosophy of the first century in Galilee, Jerusalem and elsewhere. It is a wealth of information regarding the social background at the time of Jesus. Edition quoted: (Peabody, Hendrickson, 1994)

1856 – 1861, The Athenaeum (book reviews)

The Athenaeum was a prestigious 19th century British periodical which contained articles about various literary and scholarly subjects. Book reviews were published anonymously. However, City University of London holds the original collection and has been able to identify the respective authors. Other reviewers in the Athenaeum over the years included the likes of Elizabeth Barrett Browning and Thomas Hardy. And, to get a perspective on the historical period, one of Edersheim's reviews is immediately followed by another scholar's review of Charles Dickens' latest work, *Little Dorrit*. A list of the books reviewed by Edersheim is found in Appendix C.

1858, Bohemian Reformers and German Politicians: A Contribution to the History of Protestantism

("Reformers")Thomas Constable & Co. This 60 page article comes from the book, *Essays by Ministers of the Free Church of Scotland*, edited by William Hanna. Edition cited: British Library Shelf Number: 12273. d.4. This piece focuses on the period of Church history prior to the Protestant Reformation in both Bohemia (modern day Czech Republic) and Germany. Although it is quite detailed, Ederseim said, "The reader is requested to remember that the foregoing professes to be a "Historical Essay" – not a detailed history."

1866, The Golden Diary of Heart-Converse with Jesus in the Book of Psalms

("Golden") Nisbet and Co., London. This is a devotional commentary on the book of Psalms. Fittingly, Edersheim is here at his most poetic in his descriptions of Biblical truth. Edition quoted: (Jerusalem, Keren Ahava Meshihit, 2000)

1868 – 1870, The Scattered Nation

This Hebrew Christian periodical was edited in London by Dr. Charles Schwartz. Contributors included Franz Delitzch, Adolph Saphir and A. Bernstein. Edersheim contributed a short series in 1868 called *Jewish Notes on the New Testament*, which focused on the Apostle James and the community of Jewish believers in Jesus in Jerusalem during the early years of the Church. In 1869 and 1870, Edersheim serialized a novel called *From Grey to Dawn: A Tale of Jewish Life in the Time of Christ*. It features a young man (Marcos) who travels from Alexandria, Egypt to Jerusalem for the Passover in approximately the year 30 AD. He meets several people who tell him of a Prophet from Nazareth who has been doing amazing things and gaining quite a following. The narrative is rife with descriptions of first century places and practices in typical Edersheim fashion. However, as a work of fiction, we also read first-person accounts of the events (for longer quotes, see Appendix B). For some reason, the story ends abruptly after chapter nineteen. The publication continued but this story did not. Copies of The Scattered Nation periodical are available at the National Library of Israel, and in a special collection at the Caspari Center for Biblical and Jewish Studies in Jerusalem.

1869, On Certain Peculiarities of the Jewish Race

("Peculiar") The title of this article is a good example of 19th century language. Today, the same piece would probably be called, "The Uniqueness of the Jewish People." There is a mention of it in one of Edersheim's books (OT, p. 231 – where it is incorrectly cited as "On Certain Physical Peculiarities of the Jewish Race") and it appeared in the periodical called Sunday Magazine. It offers facts and statistics about the Jewish communities of the world at the time. Edition Cited: Sunday Magazine, 1869, edited by Thomas Guthrie.

1871, Robbie and His Mother

("Robbie") Religious Tract Society, London. This is a short novel. It is less complex than his later fiction, and to the modern reader it may appear trite. At the start, the reader learns that a young boy (Robbie) and his (unnamed) mother are in a poor house, presumably in London. Robbie's sister had died and his father's whereabouts were unknown. One day a woman gives a tract to Robbie that was titled simply, "God Loves You" and included the verse John 3:16. His mother had been a woman of faith prior to entering the poor house. Robbie wondered if God loved them less now that they were poor. He realizes that God still loves them very much and he and his mother renewed their faith in God. Later, Robbie's father comes into the picture, having been in Australia working and subsequently gaining wealth. The family is now complete: the father has returned, they all have faith and their financial troubles are ended. Edition cited: British Library Shelf number: 4413.q.16.

1872, The Home and Synagogue of the Modern Jew

("Modern")Religious Tract Society, London. One source on the internet (http://chi.gospelcom.net/DAILYF/2003/03/daily-03-16-2003.shtml) attributed this book to Alfred Edersheim, and I was able to find an original version in a used book store. In the book, no author is listed by name, although all the other factors seem to indicate that Edersheim wrote (or possibly co-wrote) this book. The subtitle is: *Sketches of Modern Jewish Life and Ceremonies*. It is written for Christians to better understand some of the Jewish customs – particularly the feasts – as they are observed in various places around the globe (specifically in Europe and the Middle East). The anonymous author is described in the Preface as one who has "peculiarly favorable opportunities for becoming accurately acquainted with the customs and ritual of the Jewish Church [meaning the synagogue] of the present day. These customs he has related in the style of an eye-witness; though for several of the facts now laid before the reader, he has been indebted to the observation of others."

1872 Miriam Rosenbaum, A Story of a Jewish Life

("Rosenbaum") Religious Tract Society, London. This is a novel about the family reactions towards a Jewish person who comes to faith in Jesus. It takes place in Austria, but could just as well have been set in Victorian London. The plot: Mrs. Rosenbaum lives with her son, Levi, and his son, Anshel. The reader learns that they had relocated there several years earlier because Mrs. Rosenbaum's late husband had been thrown out of the synagogue in their previous city. The reasons for this are at first hidden, but it seems to have something to do with a book he had in his possession. Mrs. Rosenbaum also has a daughter named Miriam. Although she lived in the same town, Miriam had been shut out of their lives because she had embraced the Christian faith and married a man who became the local minister. The story is rife with accounts of the bigotry – on both sides – which exist in this ancient conflict.

As the story unfolds, both Mrs. Rosenbaum and Levi are challenged to consider the person and message of Jesus. There is the intense struggle between one's belief and one's people. Also, Miriam's young son, also named Levi, is dying from an undisclosed disease. There is family reconciliation. Before young Levi dies, he becomes one of the main instruments to share the love of Jesus with his grandmother. At the end, Mrs. Rosenbaum and her son both come to know the Saviour. The reason for Miriam's father's banishment is eventually discovered. He had become a follower of Jesus, as learned by a final letter of his that was opened and read by the family. In the afterward, we read that even young Anshel accepted the faith and desired to be a missionary to his own Jewish people.

The preface lists three questions this book seeks to address: *"What are the real thoughts of the more enlightened Jews in our days concerning Christ and Christianity? And why, when Jews are so tolerant and generous towards their Christian neighbours, so kind, and so warm in their affections, do they follow with such rancorous hatred those of their own number who have professed faith in Christ, imputing to them, almost uniformly, only the lowest and vilest motives? To these a third question may be added, as to the manner in which the truth of the gospel will sometimes at first present itself to the educated Jewish intellect."*

1873, True to the End

("True") This novel chronicles the life of a brother and sister who are orphaned in Scotland. Their Christian faith is tested and stretched as they face various trials. With dialogue often written in Scottish slang, some character names include Euphemia Bockins, Mr. Puggins, Baillie Rummelhead and Miss Caroline MacMouseland. The story has nothing to do with Jewish people or the Jewishness of Jesus. Yet, Edersheim – being who he was – used several illustrations which alluded to Jewish topics. For example: "Whether or not, like many other traits in Scottish everyday life, it forms one of those strange coincidences between the Scottish and the Jewish character, which so forcibly strike the observer, certain it is that, among at least one class of the population, the female is [favored] as compared with the male portion of a family," p. 21. Speaking of the Scottish interest in learning and their love of books, he says it is "another of those national characteristics by which the Scottish and the Jewish mind seem so closely assimilated," p. 93. Referring to the joy of a quiet Saturday night in a typical Scottish home, he says, "in this also almost imitating the Jews." (p. 321). Edition quoted: (London, John F. Shaw and Co.)

1873, What is Her Name?

("Name") Religious Tract Society, London. This is a shorter novel about a young Christian girl (Mary) who is adopted by an elderly Jewish man (Abraham Lazarus) in London. Along with some plot twists, she learns that her Savior is King of the Jews. He discovers that her Savior is also the long awaited Jewish Messiah. Edition quoted: (Waverly, P.A., Lamplighter Publishing, 2002)

1874, The Temple, its Ministry and Services

("Temple") Religious Tract Society, London. This classic book remains a valuable tool to help understand the rituals and history of the priesthood, the festivals, and the entire sacrificial system of ancient Israel. Edition quoted: (Peabody, Hendrickson, 1994)

1887, Israel's Watchman

("Watchman") Edersheim was the editor of this Hebrew Christian periodical for at least most of 1887 and possibly longer. Each monthly publication contained approximately thirty pages. Typical articles ranged from Messianic prophecies, eschatology, testimonies of Jews who came to faith in Jesus, updates on the Jewish community around the world, and the land of Palestine. British Library Shelf number: P.P.954.cc

1882, Elisha the Prophet

("Elisha") Religious Tract Society, London. A devotional commentary, this book focuses on issues of faith and service of the believer, based on the life of the prophet. It is as much of a discipleship guide as an exposition of the book of 2 Kings. Edition Quoted: *Practical Truths from Elisha*, (Grand Rapids, Kregel Publications, 1982)

1884, The Life and Times of Jesus the Messiah

("LTJM") Longman's Publishing, London. This classic work took seven years to write. It was originally published in two volumes, and a few years later there was an abridged version published in a single volume as well. It remains one of the best (if not *the* best) commentaries on the Life of Christ written in English. It contains nineteen appendices, including a twenty page list of Old Testament passages which the ancient Rabbis applied to the Messiah. Also in the Appendix is his translation and commentary of *Sefir Yetsirah* ("Book of Formation"), the earliest known Hebrew manuscripts dealing with mysticism. Edition quoted: (Peabody, Hendrickson, 1993)

His Bibliography

1876 – 1887, Bible History, Old Testament

("OT") Religious Tract Society, London. This narrative description of Old Testament history was originally published as seven separate volumes: *1. The World before the Flood and the History of the Patriarchs, 2. The Exodus and the Wanderings in the Wilderness, 3. Israel in Canaan under Joshua and the Judges, 4. Israel Under Samuel, Saul, and David, to the Birth of Solomon 5. History of Judah and Israel from the Birth of Solomon to the Reign of Ahab, 6. The History of Israel and Judah from the Reign of Ahab to the Decline of the Two Kingdoms, 7. The History of Israel and Judah from the Decline of the two Kingdoms to the Assyrian and Babylonian Captivity*; Edition quoted: (Peabody, Hendrickson, 1995)

1885, On a Theory of the Origin and Composition of the Synoptic Gospels by G. Wetzel

("Synoptic") Clarendon Press, Oxford. This essay appeared in *Studia Biblica: Essays in Biblical Archaeology and Criticism and kindred subjects by Members of the University of Oxford*, Edited by S. R. Driver, William Sanday and John Wordsworth.

1885, Prophecy and History in Relation to the Messiah

("Prophecy") Longman's Publishing, London. This is also known as the Warburton Lectures, addresses given at the Chapel of Lincoln's Inn between the years 1880 – 1884. The stated purpose of this series as a whole was, "to prove the truth of reveled religion in general, and of the Christian in particular, from the completion of those prophecies in the Old and New Testaments which relate to the Christian Church, especially to the apostacy of Papal Rome." Published in the days of great liberalism and skepticism (especially from the German school of Higher Criticism), these lectures offer an apologetic in defense of the reliability of the Scriptures and the Messiahship of Jesus. Edition quoted: (Eugene, Wipf and Stock Publishers, 2005.)

1887 Dictionary of Christian Biography

("DCB") Edited by Dr. William Smith and Henry Wace, DD. Edersheim wrote the entries for *Philo* and *Josephus*.

1888, Ecclesiasticus

("Eccl") This article, along with an exegetical commentary on the Apocryphal book of Ecclesiasticus appeared in: *The Holy Bible According to the Authorised Version, with an Explanatory and Critical Commentary by Clergy of the Anglican Church. Apocrypha*, Volume II, Edited by Henry Wace., London.

1890, Tohu-Va-Vohu

("Tohu") Published a year after his death, this is a collection of "fragmentary thoughts" compiled by his daughter, Ella. The title means "formless and void," taken from Genesis 1:2. This is the best source for getting his personal opinions on a variety of subjects.

In addition to the above, he also translated and edited books by German scholars:

1854, *The Historical Development of Speculative Philosophy from Kant to Hegel*, by H.M. Chalybaus.

1859, *Theological and Homiletical Commentary on the Gospel of St. Matthew*, by Johann Peter Lange

1860, *The History of the Christian Church to the Reformation*, by Johann Kurtz. Along with translating this work, Edersheim added the remaining history, "From the Reformation to the Present Time."

His Legacy

In the days when Edersheim wrote, it was an increasingly new and profound idea among Jews to re-inhabit the land of their forefathers. He died just eight years before Theodore Herzl called the first Zionist Congress in 1897. It was fifty nine years after his death that the nation of Israel was reborn. Yet, Edersheim had an unyielding commitment to the reality of a future for Israel. It was not wishful thinking, but simply his understanding and trust of the scriptures. Based on God's promise to Abraham and the later words of the great Hebrew prophets, a Jewish return to the Land was seen as a guarantee. And in conjunction with this, Edersheim believed whole-heartedly in the turning of his people to God's true Messiah.

> *The land and the people God has joined together; and though now the one lies desolate, like a dead body, and the other wanders unresting, as it were a disembodied spirit, God will again bring them to each other in the days when His promise shall be finally established.*[1]

The 19th century witnessed more than just the roots of Zionism. The Jewish community as a whole in Europe was undergoing a renaissance (Haskala) of its own. The writings of Moses Mendelssohn and others at the end of the 18th century paved the way for what would become Reform Judaism. Likewise, there was a new freedom in Europe for Jews to study in Universities. Previously this had been forbidden. There was also an undeniable wave of Jews coming to faith in Jesus as Messiah. They were known as Hebrew Christians, an extremely important link in the historic chain of Jews who have believed in Jesus throughout the ages. Edersheim's own definition of a Hebrew Christian is as follows:

> *Our position is this: Confessing with full heart and conviction Jesus Christ as Messiah promised to the fathers, and as our Saviour, we take our stand as members of that Church, which is equally com-*

---

1. OT, 59

posed of Jews and Gentiles. In this respect there is no distinction between Jew and Gentile; no difference in faith, hope, or love; no higher or lower standpoint. But nationally we are Hebrews, nor can our Christianity be supposed in any sense to break these ties. Israel's past history is ours; Israel's promises are ours, we share the hope of Israel. And even so far as regards the present we are intensely Jewish – Jewish in all our views, affections, and sympathies.[2]

There are numerous scholarly works, going back to the 1600s, which focus on Jewish followers of Jesus in the first few centuries of Christianity.[3] One of the first attempts at writing the complete history of Jewish believers was made by Hugh Schonfield in 1936. An eclectic Jewish scholar, Schonfield originally considered himself a follower of Jesus and called himself a "Nazarene." However, he later rejected the basic doctrines of New Testament faith, and in the 1960s wrote the famous and controversial book, *The Passover Plot*. Despite his later eccentricities, his *History of Jewish Christianity* remains a valuable resource. Regarding the rise of 19th century Hebrew Christians he said,

> The emancipation of the Jews also brought with it the emancipation of the Jewish Christian. No longer need he deny his race, but could openly proclaim himself for what he was.[4]

In London, organizations like the London Jews Society and the Mildmay Mission to the Jews helped make nineteenth century England the world leader in this endeavor. They even had a Hebrew Christian Prime Minister (Benjamin Disraeli) in 1868, and again from 1874 – 1880. Other noted Hebrew Christians included David Baron and Moses Mendelssohn's grandson, Felix, the great composer. Such were the times in which Alfred Edersheim lived and wrote. The response of the traditional Jewish community has always been the same: the assumption that Jews who embrace Christianity are only doing so for ulterior motives, or because they are rejecting Judaism. And indeed, this was quite a common phenomenon in 19th century England.[5]

2. Watchman, March 1877, p. 2

3. Paget, James Carleton, "The Terms *Jewish Christian* and *Jewish Christianity* in the History of Research," in Skarsaune, Oskar and Hvalvik, Reidar, *Jewish Believers in Jesus: The Early Centuries* (Peabody, Hendrickson, 2007), p. 22-52

4. Schonfield, Hugh, *The History of Jewish Christianity* (Duckworth, London, 1936), p. 36

5. Endelman, Todd M., *Jewish Apostasy in the Modern World* (NY, Holmes and Meier, 1987)

His Legacy

But there were also many Jews in England and other parts of Europe who turned to Christianity for a different reason. They truly believed that Jesus is the one promised by Moses and the Jewish Prophets. And for these Jews – just like today – there was usually a great price to be paid. While we do not have personal examples from Edersheim's life, he did write of this in some of his stories (see quotes below, "Jewish Views of Jewish Christians"), which are almost certainly based on personal accounts. This reality is often overlooked by the skeptics. It is also not true that "those converts who chose Christianity out of complete identification with its principles became the greatest enemies and persecutors of Judaism, just like their medieval counterparts."[6] The Hebrew Christian movement actually helped Gentile Christians begin to understand the Jewishness of Jesus, as well as God's plan for Israel. This was one way to distinguish genuine believers from others who "converted" for personal gain. One rabbi who did acknowledge the real faith of at least some of these believers was Max Heller. "No one," he wrote in a 1925 article about apostates, "has ever called in question the sincere Christian faith of Neander, Edersheim or Veit."[7]

In the twentieth century the term 'Hebrew Christian' was eventually changed to 'Jewish Christian,' as the designation 'Hebrew' began to be seen as antiquated. Still later, the term 'Messianic Jew' would make its appearance. The 'Jesus Revolution' of the late 1960s and early 1970s in the U.S. led to a bonafide revival among the Jewish people, fueling the Messianic movement we know today.[8]

The great Hebrew Christian development of the nineteenth century was a special gift to the entire body of believers in Jesus. For the Church at large, it powerfully reminds us of the Jewish roots of our faith. This truth was sadly lost for most of the Church's existence. To the modern community of Messianic Jews, on the other hand, the Hebrew Christians are our spiritual forefathers. They helped set the course. And there has

---

6. Ben-Sasson, H.H. (editor), *A History of the Jewish People* (Cambridge, Harvard University Press, 1976), p. 827

7. Heller, Max, "The Quandry of the Apostate Jew," B'nei B'rith magazine, January 1925

8. Schiffman, Michael, *Return of the Remnant* (Messianic Jewish Resources International, 1996); Rausch, David, *Messianic Judaism: Its History, Theology and Polity* (NY, Edwin Mellon Press, 1982)

recently been a rise in interest in studying the history of Jews who have believed in Jesus.[9]

Edersheim and his contemporaries were dealing with many of the same issues as today's Messianic movement. There are also some big differences. Even their language sounds foreign to the 21st century Jew who believes in Jesus. The word Yeshua (Jesus), for example, was not part of their everyday vocabulary. And their use of such words as "Jehovah," "Jewess," "convert" and "Christ" would be all but unrecognizable to most modern day Jewish believers. Before World War II, Jewish believers were simply not wrestling with questions of Jewish identity. Today, common questions in the movement include not only, "how Jewish *can* we be?" but, "how Jewish *should* we be?"[10] These are important issues which will take time to debate and clarify. But, whichever way the Messianic movement develops or splinters, we would be greatly amiss to neglect the teachings and witness of those who came before us. One contemporary Messianic leader said the following regarding Jewish believers of the 19th and early 20th centuries.

> To affix the label *Hebrew Christian* – and in doing so imply that the Jewish believers had renounced their Jewish identities – is based upon false assumptions. They were called *Hebrew Christians*, as that was the terminology of the day. However, the strength of their Jewish identity cannot be questioned. To imply otherwise ignores the modern history of our movement and diminishes the testimony of those who died in the Holocaust as Jews and as believers in Jesus.[11]

Even amongst this special group, Alfred Edersheim was unique. His writings have impacted the Church at large. His very life is also a major challenge to those in the Jewish community who say that only uneducated Jews come to profess faith in Jesus! And his legacy is a reminder that ex-

---

9. See for example, Kjaer-Hansen, Kai, Joseph *Rabinowitz and the Messianic Movement: The Herzl of Jewish Christianity* (Eerdman's 1994)

10. Goldberg, Louis, *How Jewish is Christianity?: Two Views on the Messianic Movement* (Zondervan, 2001), Cohn-Sherbock, Dan, *Voices of Messianic Judaism: Confronting Critical Issues Facing a Maturing Movement* (Messianic Jewish Resources International, 2001);

11. Glaser, Mitch, "The Traditional Jewish Mission as a Model," in *Voices of Messianic Judaism*, p. 169

amining the "Jewish roots" of the Bible is not exactly a new phenomenon. Jacob Gartenhaus said this:

> Edersheim therefore became one of the world's greatest teachers through the rich and powerful influence of his books. It was his delight to set down and to show how all Jewish hopes were fulfilled in Christ. To the end he remained as intense and brilliant a Jew as he was a profound and faithful Christian.[12]

---

12. Gartenhaus, 78

His Magnum Opus

The Life and Times of *Jesus the Messiah* has truly earned the right to be called a classic. Today, over one hundred and twenty years after its publication, it remains a favorite on the shelves of seminary libraries and Christian bookstores around the world. It has been translated into several languages (including Arabic!!). Yet, when it was first published not everyone thought it would have such a lasting impact. In 1885 one reviewer in the British periodical called The Expositor said the following:

> Dr. Edersheim is not likely to prove a formidable rival either to Dr. Gelkie or to Canon Farrar in veracity and style, or in insight into the meaning of the things which Jesus said and did; but whatever aide can be gained from the study of rabbinical writings and knowledge of Jewish habits of thoughts and modes of life, are here offered with an unrivalled abundance.[1]

Shortly after its publication it was reviewed by Emil Schurer in Germany's most prestigious theological journal. Schurer himself would publish a major work on a similar subject just a few years later.[2] He came from the more liberal, critical school of Biblical scholarship (for Edersheim's response to this approach, see the category below called "Higher Criticism"). Still, Schurer recognized that "the chief value of this book without question is the rich information which the writer gives about the Jewish relations that are influencing the life of Jesus." (author's translation)[3]

In 1921 there was a tribute in a more creative form. One writer put together a piece called *the Last Passover Night*,[4] which interpreted some of

---

1. Cited in Mayhhew, 188

2. Schurer, Emil, *A History of the Jewish People in the Time of Christ* (Edinburgh, T. and T. Clark, 1890)

3. Schurer, Emil, Review of The Life and Times of Jesus the Messiah, in Theologische Literatureitung, February 20, 1886, [Edited by Adolph Harnack and Emil Schurer]

4. Temple, William Henry, *The Last Passover Night* (London, S.P.C.K., 1921)

His Magnum Opus

the pages of *Life and Times* to be performed as a drama. Another interesting review came from Shailer Mathews, dean of the Divinity School of the Chicago University. He said that although the book "suffers from an excess of pietism, his work is not only masterly but invaluable. If one were to own but one life of Jesus, it should be Edersheim's."[5]

At about the same time, the Jewish community as a whole also began interacting with the Jewishness of Jesus and the New Testament. One important volume in this wave was Joseph Klausner's book, *Jesus of Nazareth*, which was originally written in Hebrew in 1922.[6] Several times in this work he cites Edersheim's book about the Temple, clearly acknowledging Edersheim's expertise as a scholar of the period. Ironically, he does not use – or at least did not mention – *The Life and Times of Jesus the Messiah* as a source. Unfortunately, most of the other books about Jesus from within the Jewish community have equally neglected to contend with this classic work.

One Jewish scholar who did take the time to interact with Edersheim's work was Rabbi Solomon Schecter (1847–1915). Schecter was one of the architects of Conservative Judaism in America and served as the second President of the Jewish Theological Seminary in New York City. One of his famous collections of writings is called *Studies in Judaism*, which was published in three separate volumes. The third and final series contains an article about Christian scholarship and the Talmud, and there is a section which offers a critique of *The Life and Times of Jesus the Messiah*.

Schechter found fault with Edersheim's use of Talmudic passages. "Dr. Edersheim," he wrote, "has apparently searched the Talmud diligently, but has done so with a mind preoccupied. He has arduously ransacked it for "contrasts," and has found them by misunderstanding some parts of it, and by neglecting others."[7] This is an interesting statement coming from someone who famously broke away from traditional (Orthodox) Judaism. Indeed, the history of Rabbinic thought is nothing if not a series of debates and arguments over interpretations. Schechter offers no actual comments about Jesus or the New Testament itself. He was dealing with a

---

5. Mathews, Shailer, The Biblical World, Vol. VI, p. 528, cited in Einspruch, Henry, *When Jews Face Christ* (Baltimore, The Mediator, 1932).

6. Klausner, Joseph, *Jesus of Nazareth* (MacMillan, 1925).

7. Schechter, Solomon, *Studies in Judaism, third series*, (Philadelphia, Jewish Publication Society, 1924), p. 191.

very small aspect of Edersheim's work. He did, however, say the following about *The Life and Times of Jesus the Messiah*.

> The book is one eminently designed to attract attention. Not only is the subject one of superlative interest to the education and religious world, but the evident conviction and fervent faith of the author give it a persuasiveness difficult to resist.[8]

Finally, there is also a brand new book which comes from an unlikely perspective. It is written by a Mormon woman who describes herself as a fan, and even uses the word "groupie" of Edersheim. It is the first full volume in print to focus on Alfred Edersheim, and it emphasizes his writings about Jesus.[9] Specifically, the author documents the history of Mormon writers who have quoted Edersheim in books and conference papers over the last one hundred plus years. Apparently, he is very popular in these circles as an historian. But, of course, the Mormons do not always agree with him – especially on theological issues which have traditionally kept Mormons distinct from historic Christianity. For example, the author believes that since Edersheim did not have the opportunity to learn of God's "latter day revelation" (meaning the Mormon teachings), he is now in the afterlife learning such things at the feet of Mormon scholars.[10] This affection for Edersheim is ironic. He was an historian as well as a theologian and linguist. He knew the importance of historical documentation to verify theological truths (see quotes below, for example, under the heading "Resurrection of Jesus"). The alleged miracles of Mormonism are said to have occurred during Edersheim's lifetime. Yet, they remain undocumented and without historical verification. Mormons will usually say these events should be accepted merely on faith. But if this is the case, why be so enamored with such a great historian? If nothing else, this again shows the broad reach of his scholarship.

---

8. Ibid, p. 164

9. Richardson, Marianna Edwards, *Alfred Edersheim: A Jewish Scholar for the Mormon Prophets* (Springville, Cedar Fort, 2008)

10. Ibid, p. 33

His Quotes

Abraham

WITH ABRAHAM AN ENTIRELY new period may be said to begin. He was to be the ancestor of a new race in whom the Divine promises were to be preserved, and through whom they would finally be realized.[1]

Abrahamic Covenant

FOR THE TERMS OF this promise were not made void by the seventy years which Judah spent in the captivity of Babylon, nor yet are they annulled by the eighteen centuries of Israel's present unbelief and dispersion. The promise of the land is Abram's "seed for ever." [2]

THERE IS NOTHING NARROW or particularistic, but a grand universalism, even about this presentation of the promise in concrete form.[3]

THE GREAT PROMISE CONNECTED first with the patriarchs as God's anointed, and then with Israel as a royal nation, now attached itself to Israel's king, and became, so to speak, individualized in David and his seed.[4]

FOR WHEN GOD BOUND up the future of all nations in the history of Abraham and his seed (Gen. 12:3), He made that history prophetic; and each event and every rite became, as it were, a bud, destined to open in

1. OT, 52
2. OT, 59
3. Prophecy, 44
4. Prophecy, 187

blossom and ripen into fruit on that tree under the shadow of which all nations were to be gathered.⁵

Affliction

AND WHEN TROUBLES ARE around, and we see no way of escape, when our consciences condemn us for backsliding from the Lord, what comfort to discover that the precious Word of God is still near us, with its message of pity and forgiveness, ever meeting our wants.⁶

GOD'S PEOPLE ARE NOT preserved from the common evils of this world. They are sustained and helped in them.⁷

EVEN A HEATHEN POET speaks of the pleasure of looking back upon past trials. Yet, would we rather look upon a present Saviour than a past affliction.⁸

LITTLE DO THEY KNOW, who wonder at the afflictions of God's people, what precious lessons have been learned, what mighty sermons have been preached in sick rooms and on death-beds. The letting down through the roof of the bed which bore the poor paralytic, laying him at the feet of Jesus, was itself a testimony more powerful than many a long life.⁹

Agnostics

I BELIEVE IN A personal God; I also believe in a personal Satan. Agnosticism on the latter point seems to me to lay us open to the most serious practical dangers.¹⁰

5. Temple, 163
6. Elisha, 72
7. Elisha, 117
8. Golden, 135
9. Elisha, 310
10. Tohu, 85

His Quotes

Alexandrian Judaism

SEPARATED FROM THEIR BRETHREN of Palestine, they constituted an almost independent sect, having their rival high-priest and temple. Left to themselves, and set free from those elements which led to the development of Rabbinism in the mother country, the Alexandrian Jews pursued a different direction. They had to defend their faith from the attacks of a philosophical system apparently related to it, but claiming for those initiated in its mysteries a higher spirituality and a loftier elevation.[11]

THERE CAN BE NO doubt that, in the providence of God, the location of so many Jews in Alexandria, and the mental influence which they acquired, were designed to have an important bearing on the later spread of the Gospel of Christ among the Greek-speaking and Grecian-thinking educated world.[12]

Angels

THE MINISTRY OF His angels will only be fully understood when our eyes shall have been opened, and when we shall hold personal converse with them in another state of existence.[13]

THE ANGELS WHOM GOD sends are all good, though their commission may be judgment to bring evil upon us. As one has rightly remarked, "God sends good angels to punish evil men, while to chastise good men, evil angels claim the power."[14]

---

11. Nation, 447
12. Sketches, 190
13. Elisha, 210
14. OT, 466

Anthropology

As in the soul of man we see the ruins of what he had been before the fall, so in the legends and traditions of the various religions of antiquity we recognize the echoes of what men had originally heard from the mouth of God.[15]

Has the great maker of the machinery, to us incomprehensible in its magnitude and complication, left it to the operation of those laws which has put within its every part to regulate and check its working? If so, what of the intellectual and moral aspirations within us, of that which constitutes equally the real being of man and his dignity? What of those thoughts and hopes which we instinctively feel to be heaven-born, since we know them not to have been earth-sprung? What of high moral motives, the noble inward struggles and victories, the self-devotion and self sacrifice, the patient bearing, the trustful waiting, and holy living? Truly, we cannot believe in man without believing in God.[16]

Anti-Semitism

To me, indeed, it is difficult to associate the so-called Anti-Semitic movement with any but the lowest causes; envy, jealousy, and cupidity on the one hand; or, on the other, ignorance, prejudice, bigotry and hatred of race.[17]

As they had been oppressed by Caligula, by Nero, by Domitian, and by the whole line of pagan monarchs; so were they persecuted by a Eugenius, by a Paul, by a Caraffa, and more or less by the whole line of Popes, - by the very men who owed all their idolatrous glory to the fact that they assume to be the spiritual descendants of a Hebrew fisherman! Nay, the

---

15. OT, 14
16. Elisha, 82
17. LTJM, xvii

His Quotes

Christian Bishops of Rome even exceeded the heathen Caesars in their cruelty and inhumanity towards this people.[18]

I FEEL CONVINCED THAT the real root of anti-Semitism is depreciation of the Old Testament. If we have low opinions of the Old Testament we shall come to despise and to hate the Jews, and perhaps not unreasonably so. Love for the Old Testament leads to love for Israel.[19]

Anxiety

THERE IS NO ANXIOUS, nor nervous seeking of deliverance when faith has made its confessions to God. All that is left is to anticipate victory.[20]

AN ANXIOUS MIND IS an unbelieving mind. Full of cares is full of self.[21]

Apocrypha

THE SILENCE OF THE Apocrypha about the person of the Messiah is so strange, as to be scarcely explained by the consideration, that those books were composed when the need of a Messiah for the deliverance of Israel was not painfully felt.[22]

THE HOPE OF THE Old Testament centered in the person of the Messiah; that of the Apocrypha, in the nation of the Jews.[23]

IT IS TRUE THAT the Apocrypha preserve silence about the person of the Messiah. But this, not because the Messiah was ignored, but because it was apprehended and presented in another form. It was no longer the

---

18. Modern, 121
19. Tohu, 78
20. Golden, 16
21. Golden, 184
22. LTJM, 121
23. Prophecy, 315

person of the Messiah, but the Messianic times, which engaged the expectancy of the people.[24]

Apologetics

THE CHIEF USE OF apologetics is to answer a fool according to his folly; that is, to silence him.[25]

Apostles

TOO OFTEN WE COMMIT in our estimate the error of thinking of them exclusively as Apostles, not as disciples; as our teachers, not as His learners, with all the failings of men, the prejudice of Jews, and the unbelief natural to us, but assuming in each individual special forms, and appearing as characteristic weaknesses.[26]

Art

FOR, ART IS GOD-GIVEN, and what is God-given must be capable of being in turn devoted to God. But how can this be done? The consecration of art, which is the highest expression of mind, is itself an act of homage.[27]

NOT TO PRODUCE RELIGIOUS feelings, but to express it, is the province of true art. Again, art calms and elevates the mind, and, if it takes us to its own high altitude, that there we may pray and worship, another of its objects is fulfilled.

---

24. Prophecy, 316
25. Tohu, 20
26. LTJM, 545
27. Elisha, 77

His Quotes

POETRY AND MUSIC HAVE always been favorite engagements with Israel, and originality peculiarly their own, and peculiarly expressive of their national mental characteristics.[28]

SPEAKING AS ONE WHO has no claim to knowledge of art, only one picture of Christ ever really impressed me. It was that of an 'Ecce Homo,' by Carlo Dolei, in the Pitti Gallery at Florence.[29]

ART, LIKE SCRIPTURE, HAS this for its object: to make us see, through the actual and outward, the spiritual and therefore the truly real. It presents reality, but as that through which we look far away into the ideal, which underlies all, surrounds all, and gives meaning to all.[30]

Atheism

SELF INDULGENCE AND COVETOUSNESS are practical atheism.[31]

AT THE ROOT OF all evil, deep in our hearts, is atheism.[32]

IT DESERVES MORE THAN passing notice, that the modern denial of God may be reduced to the same ultimate principle as the worship of Baal. For, if the great First Cause – God – God as the Creator – be denied, then the only mode of accounting for the origin of all things is to trace it to the operation of forces in matter. And what really is this but a deification of nature.[33]

28. Nation 350
29. LTJM, 176
30. Tohu, 55
31. Golden, 65
32. Golden, 92
33. OT, 690

For, we confidently assert and challenge experiment of it, that disbelief in a God, or materialism, involves infinitely more difficulties, and that at every step and in regard to all things, than the faith of the Christian.[34]

For myself, I cannot understand the rascaldom which underlies writings and lectures intended to make men atheists. If everything is only mud – including, of course, such writings and arguments – what can be the purpose of them? Only that of self-display, and, for myself, I do not admire even the largest accumulation of mud standing out from circumnatant [sic] mud.[35]

Atonement

On the shedding of blood, which was of the greatest importance – since, according to the Talmud, 'whenever the blood touches the altar the offerer is atoned for' – followed the 'flaying' of the sacrifice and the 'cutting up into his pieces.' All this had to be done in an orderly manner, and according to certain rules, the apostle adopting the sacrificial term when he speaks of 'rightly dividing the word of truth' (2 Timothy 2:15).[36]

But even the need of such a Day of Atonement, after the daily offerings, the various festive offerings, and the private and public sin-offerings all the year round, showed the insufficiency of all such sacrifices, while the very offerings of the Day of Atonement proclaimed themselves to be only temporary and provisional, 'imposed until the time of reformation.'[37]

The sin-offering – This is the most important of all sacrifices. It made atonement for the *person* of the offender, whereas the trespass-offering only atoned for one special offence . . . However, in reference to [both of them], the Rabbinical principle must be kept in view – that they only atoned in case of real repentance.[38]

34. LTJM, 689
35. Tohu, 68
36. Temple, 84
37. Temple, 241
38. Temple, 94

His Quotes

Babylonian Exile

It were a one sided view to regard the Babylonish exile as only punishment for Israel's sin. There is, in truth, nothing in all God's dealings in history exclusively *punitive*. That were a merely negative element. But there is always a positive element also of actual progress; a step forward, even though in the taking of it something should have to be crushed. And this step forward was the development of the Kingdom of God in its relation to the world.[39]

Bar Kochba

His designation as Bar Cochab (the son of a star) dates from his claims to be the long-promised Messiah, and the application to him of the prophetic passage in Numbers 24:17 . . . It is indeed indescribably sad to see a man, weighed down under the burden of years, and endowed with the earnestness, enthusiasm, and generosity of an Akiba, support the claims of so vulgar and clumsy an imposter as Bar Cochab, or Bar Cosab (the son of a lie), as his disappointed followers called him at a later period.[40]

Such was the Messiah of Israel's choice, whom they now prepared to support. Only one party in the land opposed a passive resistance to the "son of a lie." It is touching to have again and again to chronicle the trials, the patience, and the faith of the Jewish Christians. This small and despised number of disciples neither could nor would own the deceiver's claims.[41]

---

39. LTJM, 114
40. Nation, 217
41. Nation, 219

Belief

THERE IS NOT A more common, nor can there be a more fatal mistake in religion or religious movements than to put confidence in mere negations, or to expect from them lasting results for good. A negation without a corresponding affirmation – indeed, if it is not the outcome of it – is of no avail for spiritual purposes. We must speak, because we believe; we deny that which is false only because we affirm and cherish the opposite truth.[42]

Belonging to God

WE ARE GOD'S PROPERTY: blood-bought, love-sought, and Spirit-brought.[43]

THE MEANEST OF GOD'S saints *is* one of God's saints.[44]

I MUST REMEMBER THAT holiness is the badge of adoption. God not only takes us to be His children, but makes us to be His children.[45]

THE LORD GIVES US not only adoption, but 'the spirit of adoption,' the family likeness with the family privileges, and not merely the name but the character of children.[46]

IF WE REGARD ANYTHING as our own, then surely *all* is still our own, and we are not His who bought us with His precious blood.[47]

---

42. OT, 844
43. Golden, 22
44. Golden, 113
45. Golden, 130
46. Golden, 226
47. Golden, 242

His Quotes

THERE IS INFINITE COMFORT and hope even in the fact of being God's creature – the work of His Hand.[48]

Bethlehem

SHELTERED FROM SCENES OF strife and semi-heathenism, the little village of Bethlehem had retained among its inhabitants the purity of their ancestral faith and the simplicity of primitive matters. Here, embosomed amidst the hills of Judah, where afterwards David pastured his father's flocks, and where shepherds heard angels hail the birth of "David's greater Son," we seem to feel once again the healthful breath of Israel's spirit, and we see what moral life it was capable of fostering alike in the individual and in the family.[49]

Binding of Isaac (Genesis 22)

AS WE REMEMBER THAT on this mountain-top the temple of the Lord afterwards stood, and that from it rose the smoke of accepted sacrifices, we can understand all the better what the inspired writer adds by way of explanation: As it is said to this day, "In the mount where Jehovah is seen," – where he seeth and is seen, - whence also the name of *Moriah* is derived.[50]

UPON ISAAC, ALSO, THE event had a most important bearing. For when he resisted not his father, and allowed himself to be bound and laid on the altar, he entered into the spirit of Abraham, he took upon himself his faith, and thus showed himself truly the heir to the promises.[51]

48. Tohu, 1
49. OT, 391
50. OT, 72
51. OT, 72

Blessings

AND THE EXPERIENCE OF mercy received in the past is pledge of mercies to be received in the future . . . a prayer heard in the past is pledge of prayers to be heard in the future. Each blessing we receive is but one link; a link fastened on to other links, the whole forming the chain of sovereign love by which Christ binds a soul unto Himself.[52]

WE ARE NEITHER TO be indifferent to earthly blessings, nor to be dependent upon them for our happiness. But we are to trust our Father, alike when He gives and when He withholds, and still to rejoice in Him.[53]

BUT THE INTERPOSITION OF God, although direct, is not of the nature of magic. If any success granted by Him is to be complete, it implies moral conditions on our part. To put it otherwise: the full reception of God's benefits has for its condition full receptivity on the part of man.[54]

Blood Atonement

IN ACCORDANCE WITH THIS [Leviticus 17:11] we quote the following Jewish interpreters. Rashi says: 'The soul of every creature is bound up in its blood; therefore I gave it to atone for the soul of man – that one should come and atone for the other.' Similarly, Iben Ezra writes: 'One soul is a substitute for the other.' And Moses Ben Nachmann: "I gave the soul for you on the altar, that the soul of the animal should be an atonement for the soul of the man."[55]

---

52. Elisha, 266
53. Elisha, 271
54. OT, 858
55. Temple, 86

His Quotes

Burdens

It is not the burden which weighs us down; it is when we have to bear it alone, and *so long* as we bear it alone.[56]

To lay our case before Him is to be already relieved. The burden which I have rolled upon Him can no longer bear me down; it has ceased to be *my* burden.[57]

And, in truth, there is only one burden which is really heavy to bear – that of sin. Every other burden – that of sorrow, of want, or of difficulty – drives us straight to God. This alone seems to keep us from God.[58]

A man from whom a burden has been lifted feels happier even then he who has never known its weight.[59]

There is something wonderfully soothing in telling our cares and sorrows to another. The burden often loses half its weight at least when it is shared by another. But when that other, whom we trust and love, continues firm and hopeful, the whole aspect of matters seem at once changed. What formerly appeared surrounded by unknown terrors is now seen its true proportions and real light. We are inspired with fresh courage to do battle with difficulties.[60]

Canaanites

Moreover, it is very remarkable that we perceive in the Canaanite race those very things which afterwards formed the characteristics of heathen-

---

56. Golden, 2
57. Golden, 67
58. Golden, 262
59. Name, 61
60. Rosenbaum, 44

ism, as we find it among the most advanced nations of antiquity, such as Greece and Rome.[61]

VERY MUCH IN THE mythology, and almost all the vileness of Greek and Roman heathenism is undoubtedly of Canaanitish origin. Indeed, we may designate the latter as the only real *missionary* heathenism at the time in the world.[62]

"Christian" Anti-Semitism

A GREAT CRIME IS being enacted over the world, which cries to heaven for vengeance, and to the Church for testimony and self-vindication. While we speak of that salvation which is of the Jews, and of the joyous fulfillment of all promises in Christ, other thoughts obtrude themselves, and, like heavy rain clouds, crowd our horizon, and darken out the light of our gladness. For once more has the wild howl of unchained passion against Israel risen above the sweet music of the dying Saviour's last prayer: 'Father, forgive them, for they know not what they do.' Once more has the blood-stained hand of rapine, lust, and murder sought to shake from out the jeweled memorial cup, in which the Church had gathered and held up in a constant Prayer of Intercession, the tears which Jesus had shed over the Jerusalem that would not receive Him – tears, that can never be dried up. And once more has the white raiment of the Church been fouled with blood; her fair name been a byword, and her hymn of charity drown by wild orgies. The hand raised to point to the cross drops in anguish.[63]

THE CHURCH VEILS HER face in mourning; a thrill of horror, a pang of anguish, a cry of indignation pass through universal humanity. Whether and what in the wonder-working Providence of Him who brings good out of evil may be the outcome of this to Israel, we cannot say. But in the name of God, let us clear ourselves of all complicity in this sin and shame. We who do believe in Christ, and because we believe in Him, as the true Messiah – we protest with one heart and mind against this and all like

---

61. OT, 20
62. OT, 343
63. Prophecy, 157

movements! In the name of Christianity, in the name of our Church, in the name of this land of liberty and light, in the name of universal humanity, we abhor it, we denounce it, we protest against it.[64]

Christianity

IT IS THE NEW Testament which represents our Christianity, not the eccentricities nor the supposed narrow-mindedness of its pretending or even real professors.[65]

ON WHICH SIDE DOES progress in science and literature lie – on the Christian or the heathen? Where is moral grandeur exhibited – among the pagans, or by earnest believers? And what remedy would *you* propose to apply to the world's ills, what comfort to its sorrows, and what satisfaction for its cravings?[66]

CHRISTIANITY ADDRESSES ITSELF TO the inner man; the outer man, and the changes and appearances observable in it, are only the spontaneous consequences of the great change wrought within. It is indeed true, that the Gospel brings before us not only those great truths which are to make us wise unto salvation, but also the great principles of right, of virtue, and of holiness.[67]

THE FUNDAMENTAL IDEAS OF the Christian life may, we conceive, be summed up in the two words, *spiritual liberty*.[68]

IT IS A REMARKABLE fact, that in measure as less of spiritual attachment to Christianity is displayed, the intolerance which all other forms of religion are treated, becomes more bitter.[69]

64. Prophecy, 158
65. Elisha, 55
66. True, 71
67. Nation, 145
68. Nation, 146
69. Nation, 540

To put it more precisely: we hold that Christianity in its origin appealed to an existing state of expectancy, which was the outcome of a previous development; and further, that those ideas and hopes of which it professed to be the fulfillment had not first sprung up in the immediately preceding period – that is, in the centuries between the return from the Babylonish exile and the Birth of Christ – but stretched back through the whole course of Old Testament teaching.[70]

But liable as, in our present state, we are to continual error, and to none more readily than to falling into extremes, we are prone either to disassociate the element of faith from the Christian life, or the Christian life from the impelling power of a living faith. Either of these extremes leads to doctrinal error, and to practical mistakes. A genuine Christianity has to present the Christian life as based upon, derived from, and pervaded by faith – the leaven of the gospel leavening the whole lump, and Christian faith as a matter of not only intellect, but of the heart and life also.[71]

Christianity is a constant negation. Its teaching is a negation of what naturally comes to the mind; its practice a negation of what naturally presents itself to the imagination and the heart. Practical Christianity is a constant saying: 'No! no! no!' to all around – the world, the flesh, the devil – and, not unfrequently, to the so-called Church too.[72]

Christianity is always new: it has something new to say to every generation, though the new be always the old truth. And therein lies its appeal to our times.[73]

The Church

On earth, and in the present dispensation, let us not look for the one and undivided Church of Christ. Thoughts of it are like the chimes of distant bells, borne upon the breeze to the ear of the weary pilgrim. Man

---

70. Prophecy, 5
71. Reformers, 237
72. Tohu, 16
73. Tohu, 95

speaks of Churches; Christ has one Church; and when He cometh, he will not only manifest His own and His Father's glory, but also the beauty and unity of His Church.[74]

I MAY LOVE MY own church very much, but I love Christ and His church – *the* Church – still better.[75]

GENERALLY SPEAKING, THE ETERNAL history of every church passes through three phases. In the first or *constituent* period, principles are laid down and landmarks set; in the second or *formative* period, these principles are developed into rules, being extended or modified, as the case may be; in the third or *discriminative* period, all internal questions are settled, and the outward relations of the church, and with them her aims and positions, finally fixed.[76]

Circumcision

WE HAVE ALREADY SEEN that the initiatory rite of the Covenant, circumcision, was, even in the Pentateuch, presented in its symbolic aspect, and shown to point to another circumcision, that of the lips and the heart, which in the future would become a great spiritual reality to all men. It is in this view of circumcision that Moses speaks of himself as of 'uncircumcised lips,' that is, as unprepared for great spiritual work, while in Lev 26:41 we read of 'uncircumcised hearts,' and in Deuteronomy the command to circumcise the heart is explained as equivalent to being 'no more stiff-necked.'[77]

Constantine

ALTHOUGH CONSTANTINE HAD ALL along professed his allegiance to Christianity, and so far advanced its cause, discouraging all heathen prac-

74. Golden, 48
75. Golden, 307
76. Reformers, 239
77. Prophecy, 168

tices, it cannot be denied that in his conduct he exhibited few if any of the Christian graces.[78]

His religion was the popular Christianity of his period, a zeal for the outward together with a barren faith and a conformity to superstitious practices; a mass of wood, hay and stubble, in which the master's eye alone could discern whether there was any real and precious foundation.[79]

Conviction

Conviction is the knowledge and sense of our estrangement from Him.[80]

Coveting

And of all sins, covetousness perhaps is the most generally prevalent in our days. It holds not only the world in bondage, but it has affected the Church.[81]

Every other sin comes and goes, so to speak; covetousness never goes nor comes again; it is always there, and always casts over us its broad shadow.[82]

Creation

We must expect to find in the first chapter of Genesis simply the grand outlines of what took place, and not any details connected with creation. On these points there is ample room for such information as science may

---

78. Nation, 530
79. Nation, 532
80. Golden, 89
81. Golden, 67
82. Elisha, 182

be able to supply, when once it shall have carefully selected and sifted all that can be learned from the study of earth and of nature.[83]

AN ALMOST INFINITE SPACE of time, and many changes, may therefore have intervened between the *creation* of heaven and earth, as mentioned in [Genesis chapter One] ver. 1, and the chaotic state of our earth, as described in ver. 2.[84]

The Crusades

DEVOTION WITHOUT DEVOUTNESS, – feats of daring and bravery unsurpassed, but not rewarded by any lasting results, – mighty but planless and unsustained undertakings, – army after army launched on the plains of Syria, victorious yet not conquering, and still fresh supplies poured after them on the same hopeless errand – until at last the most undaunted courage is obliged to yield the field to the Infidels. Such in few words is a summary of the history known as the Crusades... Princess, lords, nobles, peasants, monks – nay, even woman – some from good, others from more doubtful motives, set out for Jerusalem.[85]

Daniel 7:13

DANIEL 7:13 IS CURIOUSLY explained in the Talmud (Sanh. 98a), where it is said that if Israel behaved worthily, the Messiah would come in the clouds of heaven; if otherwise, humble, and riding upon an ass.[86]

David

SAUL WAS THE KING after Israel's own heart (1 Sam. 12:13); David the king after God's own heart, not because of his greater piety or goodness, but

83. OT, 11
84. OT, 12
85. Athenaeum, 3/19/1859
86. LTJM, 1004

because, despite his failings and sins, he fully embodied the Divine idea of Israel's kingdom; and for this reason also he and his kingdom were the type of our Lord Jesus Christ and of His Kingdom.[87]

A YEAR HAD PASSED since David's terrible fall. The child of his sin had been born. And all this time God was silent! Yet like a dark cloud on a summer's day hung this Divine sentence over him: "But the thing that David had done was evil in the eyes of Jehovah" (2 Sam 11:27). Soon it would burst into a storm of judgment.[88]

AS ABRAHAM PERPETUATED HIS progress through the land by rearing an altar unto Jehovah in every place he sojourned, so David has chronicled every phase in his inner and outer life by a Psalm – a waymark and an altar for lone pilgrims in all ages.[89]

LEFT TO CHOOSE BETWEEN famine, defeat, and pestilence, David wisely and well cast himself upon the Lord, finding comfort only in the thought, which has so often brought relief to those who realize it, that, even when suffering for sin, it is well to fall into the hands of Jehovah.[90]

Day of Atonement

MOSES PRESCRIBES, FIRST, A high priest; secondly, a goat, whose blood was brought into the Holy of Holies; and, thirdly, a goat to be sent away: so that, where these three are wanting, the conditions required by Moses are not fulfilled, and there is therefore no atonement. Without these three things, the day itself has no virtue; and, therefore, there is really now no atonement for Israel. The assertion about the day itself is a mere invention of the Rabbis, the only value of which is to show how deeply they felt the

---

87. OT, 450
88. OT, 540
89. OT, 555
90. OT, 572

insufficiency of repentance, and the necessity of a real atonement in order to procure remission of sins.[91]

TRADITION HAS IT, THAT on the Day of Atonement no less than five hundred priests were wont to assist in the services.[92]

Death

SOME ARE AFRAID TO witness sorrow, to hear of death, even to meet a funeral procession, as if by passing over to the other side they could ever avert lengthening shadow that is creeping over them. Why not rather think of all this as a reality, and prepare for it while there is still time?[93]

Deborah

FAR AWAY IN MOUNT Ephraim God raised up a woman, on whom He had poured the spirit of prophecy. It is the first time in history that we read of the prophetic gift. The sacred text conveys, that she exercised it in strict accordance with the Divine law, for it is significantly added in connection with it, that "she judged Israel at that time." Deborah, 'the bee,' is described as a "burning woman."[94]

Defeat

ISRAEL HAD PRESUMED TO go up into this mountain-top without the presence of Jehovah, without the Ark of the Covenant, and without Moses. Yesterday they had been taught the lesson that their seeming weakness would be real strength, if Jehovah were among them. To-day they had in

---

91. Modern, 103
92. Temple, 103
93. Elisha, 118
94. OT, 351

bitter experience to find out this other and equally painful truth – that their seeming strength was real weakness.[95]

Denominations

SOME OF THESE SECTARIES may be excellent wine – but, ah me! it is dreadfully corked![96]

OUR RELIGIOUS DIFFERENCES MOSTLY spring from what all of us do not know, but pretend to know.[97]

Disappointments

WHAT WE CALL DISAPPOINTMENTS are only not God's appointments.[98]

Discipleship (walking with God)

THE LORD HAS DIED – despond not. The Lord is risen – doubt not. The Lord is exalted – fear not. The Lord reigneth – hesitate not. The Lord returneth – delay not.[99]

WHATEVER MY PAST HISTORY, or my present state and condition, my misery consists not so much in what I am, as in what I refuse to be.[100]

---

95. OT, 248
96. Tohu, 19
97. Tohu, 104
98. Tohu, 49
99. Golden, 12
100. Golden, 23

His Quotes

NEVER DID A PILGRIM set out on his way to the heavenly Jerusalem, but it seemed as if it were impossible to reach its pearly gates. Never has anything been attempted for the glory of God, but the difficulties appeared insuperable.[101]

WE ARE 'STRANGERS AND pilgrims.' Surely, not the one without the other. To be a stranger without being a pilgrim were morbid misanthropy; to be a pilgrim without being a stranger were empty profession. The one marks our relation to earth, the other our relation to heaven.[102]

ALTHOUGH THE PILLAR OF cloud was the real guide of Israel in their journeying, yet the local knowledge of Hobab would manifestly prove of the greatest use in indicating springs and places of pasturage. And so it always is. The moving of the cloud or its resting must be our sole guide; but under its direction the best means which human skill or knowledge can suggest should be earnestly sought and thankfully used.[103]

IN EVERY GREAT CRISES of history, and, we feel persuaded, in the great crises of every individual life, there is such a meeting and parting of the two ways – to life or destruction.[104]

OFTIMES OUR THOUGHTS, ALTHOUGH springing from motives of real religion, are not God's thoughts, and the lesson here conveyed is most important of not taking our own impressions, however earnestly and piously derived, as necessarily in accordance with the will of God, but testing them by His revealed word, – in short, of making our test in each case not subjective feeling, but objective reality.[105]

FOR, AT RISK OF uttering a truism, we must insist that there are only two courses possible – either to yield ourselves wholly to the guidance of the Holy Spirit, or else to follow our natural impulses. These impulses are

101. Golden, 24
102. Golden, 115
103. OT, 240
104. OT, 278
105. OT, 530

not such as we may, perhaps, imagine, or suppose them to have become under the influence of religion. For the natural man always remains what he had been – what birth, nationality, education, and circumstances has made him. This consideration should keep us from harsh and, probably, erroneous judgments of others, and may likewise serve for our own warning and instruction.[106]

AND SO IT EVER is; and therefore does every specific demand upon our faith stand between a general promise and a special assurance, that, resting upon the one, we may climb the other; and thus every specific trial – and every trial is also one of our faith – may become a fresh starting – point in the spiritual life.[107]

BUT THERE CAN BE no crown without the cross, nor will double portion of the Spirit come without the lonely walk.[108]

DISCIPLESHIP IS NOT THE result of any outward manifestation by 'evidences' or demonstration. It requires the conversion of a child-like spirit.[109]

IT IS IMPOSSIBLE FOR the disciple to make separation between spiritual matters and worldly, and to attempt serving God in the one and Mamon in the other. There is absolutely no distinction to the disciple, and our common usage of the words secular and spiritual is derived from a terrible misunderstanding and mistake. To the secular, nothing is spiritual; and to the spiritual, nothing is secular.[110]

AND THUS DISCIPLESHIP, THEN, and, in measure, to all time, involves the necessity of complete inward surrender of everything for the love of Christ, so that if, and when, the time of outward trial comes, we may be

---

106. OT, 564
107. OT, 673
108. Elisha, 17
109. LTJM, 564
110. LTJM, 666

His Quotes

prepared to conquer in the fight. He fights well, who has first fought and conquered within.[111]

TO SOME THE WAY to Christ is up the Mount of Transfiguration, among the shinning beings of another world; to some it is across dark Kedron, down the deep garden of Gethsemane with its agonies. What matter it, if it equally leads to Him, and equally brings the sense of need and experience of pardon to the seeker after the better, and the sense of need and experience of holiness to the seeker after pardon?[112]

AND, INDEED, RECEPTION OF Christ's word, knowledge of His essential nature, and faith in His Mission: such seem the three essential characteristics of those who are Christ's.[113]

Dispensations

FROM FIRST TO LAST, the two dispensations are substantially one; Jehovah, the God of Israel, is also the God and Father of our Lord and Saviour Jesus Christ.[114]

IN THE NEW TESTAMENT dispensation the outward calling is the result of, or at least intimately connected with, the inner state. The reverse was the case under the Old Testament, where the outward calling seems to mould the men. Even the prophetic office is not quite an exception to this rule.[115]

IN GENERAL, WE WILL once more thus formulate our views: *In the days of Christ men learned first to believe in His Person, and then in His Word; in*

---

111. LTJM, 686
112. LTJM, 710
113. LTJM, 840
114. Temple, xii
115. OT, 425

the dispensation of the Holy Spirit we learn first to believe in His Word, and then in His Person.[116]

AND SO IT STILL is, that the New Testament without the Old, and the Old Testament without the New, is not possible.[117]

OF OLD THERE WERE intermittent springs, now we have a perennial fountain: then the Holy Spirit fell on individuals at special times, now He dwells permanently in all His people; then there were prophets, now we have One ever-living Prophet, an everlasting link that binds us to God, One Who not only brings the promises, but in Whom they are yea and Amen.[118]

WITH HIS OWN HAND God took down the tabernacle, and closed the temple-doors: He put His seal to the termination of the Old Testament dispensation.[119]

Divorce

OUR LORD REPLIED BY pointing out that Moses had not commanded divorce, only tolerated it on account of their hardness of heart, and in such commanded to give a bill of divorce for the protection of the wife.[120]

Doctors

THE RABBIS ORDAINED THAT every town must have at least one physician, who was also to be qualified to practice surgery, or else a physician and a surgeon. Some of the Rabbis themselves engaged in medical pursuits: and, in theory at least, every practitioner ought to have had their license. To

---

116. LTJM, 426
117. Prophecy, 25
118. Prophecy, 143
119. Nation, 8
120. LTJM, 706

His Quotes

employ a heretic or a Hebrew Christian was specially prohibited, though a heathen might, if needful, be called in.[121]

Documentary Hypothesis

NO OTHER BOOK HAS ever been composed in this manner. It may be as Wellhausen says; but in that case the Pentateuch is certainly, from a literary point of view, a unique production. We know that in a composition of a work many sources may be used and various authorities quoted, yet literary history would be searched in vain for another patchwork of the kind in which half-a-dozen or more books are cut up and pieced together in so cunning a manner. Viewed as a purely literary question, the story of the Pentateuch, as told by some of these critics, is not only unparalleled, but transparently impossible.[122]

WHATEVER OBJECTIONS MAY BE raised against what is called the 'traditional' view, whatever difficulties may attach to the conciliation of the supposed differences between notices in the historical books and the enactments of the Mosaic code, the theory of Wellhausen is not the thread to lead us out of, rather that lead us into, the labyrinth.[123]

Doubt

ALL DOUBTS OF HIS grace, or of His ability or willingness to save, are of the devil.[124]

DOUBTS ARE CLOUDS WHICH, passing between Christ and our souls, hide the view of Him.[125]

    121. Sketches, 151
    122. Prophecy, 51
    123. Prophecy, 209
    124. Golden, 23
    125. Golden, 119

If there is any point on which we should anxiously be on our guard, it is that of "tempting God." We do so tempt the Lord when, listening to our own inclinations, we put once more the question that which he has already clearly settled. Where God *has* decided, never let us doubt, nor lag behind.[126]

When John [the Baptist] asked the question: Do we wait for another? Light was already struggling through the darkness. It was incipient victory even in defeat. When he sent his disciples with the question straight to Christ, he had already conquered; for such a question addressed to a possibly false Messiah has no meaning . . . The answer lies in this: whether doubt will lead us *to* Christ or *from* Christ.[127]

Ecclesiasticus

[The Book of Ecclesiasticus'] chief importance lies in this, that it exhibits Jewish thought and religion at a period otherwise almost unknown, that it connects the traditions of the past with questions of the future; and that, while embodying both, it marks the transition from the one to the other.[128]

But, far beyond this, the special claims of Ecclesiasticus may be thus briefly summed up: It is the oldest known Apocryphon; it unquestionably originated in Palestine, and was written in Hebrew, and it presents a new phase of Judaism. . . . The Greek translation in which it has come down is both historically and in point of time connected with the LXX Version of the Old Testament, and hence necessarily reflects light upon it.[129]

Even a cursory perusal of the book shews that the general moral tone of the writer is not at any time lofty. Often it is decidedly low, and his allusions become coarsely realistic.[130]

126. OT, 81
127. LTJM, 459
128. Eccl., 1
129. Eccl., 2
130. Eccl., 17

His Quotes

We have little doubt that there are passages in various parts of the New Testament in which either the sentiment or its mode of expression carries us back to Ecclesiasticus. . . . This holds specifically true in regards to the Epistle of St. James.[131]

Eighteen Benedictions

Originally the eulogies were eighteen in number. The addition of that against heretics would have made them nineteen. Accordingly, Eulogy 15, which prayed for the coming of the Branch of David, was joined to the previous one in order to preserve the number eighteen. It is sadly characteristic that, together with a curse upon Christian converts, the messianic hope of Israel should thus have been pushed into the background.[132]

Elijah

He was the impersonation of the Old Testament, in one of its aspects: that of grandeur and judgment – the living realization of the top-most height of the mount, which burned with fire around which lightnings played and thunder rolled, and from out of whose terrible glory spake the voice of Jehovah, the God of Israel.[133]

A grander figure never stood out even against the Old Testament sky than that of Elijah.[134]

---

131. Eccl., 22
132. LTJM, 306
133. OT, 668
134. OT, 668

As we recall his almost unlimited power, we remember that its spring was in constant prayer.[135]

What a contrast between those Baal-debauched Samaritans and this man; what a greater contrast still between the effeminate decrepit priests of Baal, in their white linen garments and high-pointed bonnets, and this stern prophet of Jehovah.[136]

Strange as it may seem, these felt weaknesses of men like Elijah come upon us with almost a sense of relief. It is not only that we realise that these giants of faith are men of like passions with ourselves, but that the Divine in their work is thereby the more prominently brought out.[137]

Elisha

Elijah was the precursor of St. John the Baptist; Elisha, that of our Blessed Lord and Savior Jesus Christ.[138]

Essenes

They seemed to have combined a kind of higher grade Pharisaism with devotional views, and even practices, derived from eastern mysticism, and more particularly from the Medo-Persian religion.[139]

Eternal Life

It refers not to the future, but to the present. It is the realization of what Christ had told them in these words: 'Ye believe in God, believe also in Me.' It is the pure sunlight on the soul, resulting in, or reflecting the

135. OT, 668
136. OT, 670
137. OT, 696
138. Elisha, 42
139. Sketches, 223

knowledge of Jehovah; the Personal, Living, true God, and of Him Whom He did send, Jesus Christ.[140]

Evangelism

A CHILD OF GOD is of necessity a missionary. If others speak well of what they love, how can we otherwise than 'show forth' all His 'marvelous works?'[141]

OUR RELIGION LIES NOT in withdrawal from the world, but in leavening it with the gospel.[142]

FOR WHY SHOULD WE not declare what God has done for our souls?[143]

THERE ARE THOSE WHO, even when they speak the truth, speak it almost as if it were a falsehood, or even with bated breath and humble demeanor, as if, so far as God's truth is concerned, we were not all equal. Surely there cannot be a different method of preaching to rich and to poor sinners. If we believe that our message is sent by God, then let us speak it fearlessly; if otherwise, let us forbear. Nor let the truth be put before others in such manner, as to what small amount of it is doled out can scarcely be disentangled from the misleading platitudes with which it is overlaid and enwrapped.[144]

THE MINISTERIAL WORK BRINGS with it the obligation of entire self-forgetfulness, self denial, and self-devotion. No other object, no other joy, no other engagement must occupy us, compared with that of serving the Lord in winning souls. Not to please men, but to awaken the dead, are we sent forth.[145]

140. LTJM, 839
141. Golden, 60
142. Golden, 155
143. Elisha, 21
144. Elisha, 72
145. Elisha, 111

We profess to have been redeemed through the precious blood of Christ, and yet what have we done for Him, Who has bought us at such a price, and Whose we are? We believe that the world lieth in the evil one, and that its only remedy is the Gospel, and yet what are we doing for its spread?[146]

Ah, my dear reader, if we but understood the deep soul-need of those with whom we are oft in the closest everyday contact, their poverty of spirit, and great longing for that comfort which the gospel alone can supply, should we not be less neglectful and less selfish in our dealings with them?[147]

Evolution

It is a *fact*, that infidelity has scarcely made any real advances these two thousand years; and even the latest theory of the origin of the world and of men from atoms has been propounded hundreds of years before Paul met the Epicureans and Stoics on Mars' Hill.[148]

Some modern science has carried unbelief one step nearer to the utterly irrational. What formerly was Materialism, ought now to be called Accidentalism.[149]

Ezra

In truth, Palestine owed everything to Ezra, the Babylonian, a man so distinguished that, according to tradition, the Law would have been given by him, if Moses had not previously obtained that honor.[150]

---

146. Elisha, 130
147. Name, 55
148. True, 70
149. Tohu, 52
150. LTJM, 7

His Quotes

Faith

LIVING FAITH BREATHES PRAYER; otherwise faith were a work.[151]

THAT HE IS A ROCK and a Redeemer, is His revelation in grace; that he is *my* Rock and *my* Redeemer, is my application in faith. For faith dares to write the personal pronoun into God's promises, and it does so on the warrant of God's invitation.[152]

THE MORE FAITH IS exercised, the stronger it grows.[153]

FAITH ITSELF IS MERELY an empty casket, valuable only in so far as it holds Christ.[154]

FAITH RESTS ON TWO pillars - the character of God and the promises of God.[155]

FOR FAITH IS NEVER a thing of the past.[156]

THANK GOD, WE HAVE sufficient and most firm historical ground for faith in Him, as well as the inward teaching and assurance of the Holy Ghost; sufficient, not indeed to supersede the necessity of faith, but to make that "blessed faith," so well grounded, so glorious, so joyous, and so transforming in its power, not only reasonable to us, but of obligatory duty to all men.[157]

---

151. Golden, 27
152. Golden, 162
153. Golden, 166
154. Golden, 213
155. Golden, 253
156. OT, 340
157. OT, 548

THE MOST DARING AND certain faith is not presumption. It presumes nothing; it only trusts in One Who is tried and precious.[158]

IT MAY SEEM STRANGE that we are brought into straits not only for our good, but for our happiness. And yet it is true. Surely, the happiest moment to the Christian is when, utterly unable to find any help around, he finds grace in simple faith to cast his burden upon the Lord, quite content to leave it there, and quite certain that He is faithful in Whom he has believed. The *what* and the *how* of the deliverance form no longer subject of care; he has the Lord himself as surety for good. Such exercise of faith fills the heart with intense peace and perfect calm. It is not victory, it is *rest*.[159]

SOME PEOPLE ALWAYS OSCILLATE between faith and unbelief, like the pendulum of a Dutch clock, and with the same loud and disagreeable tick.[160]

Fear

THEY WHO FEAR HAVE not well learned the blessedness of believing.[161]

WE MARK FIRST THE cowardice of the man who gives way to despair before any danger has actually arisen. Yet there are not a few who tremble not before that which is real, but before fears, which, after all, prove wholly groundless. It need scarcely be said how much good work, whether on the part of individuals or of the Church, has been hindered by apprehensions of this kind.[162]

---

158. Elisha, 24
159. Elisha, 87
160. Tohu, 125
161. Golden, 120
162. OT, 780

His Quotes

Feast of Tabernacles

We have here the only Old Testament type yet unfulfilled; the only Jewish festival which has no counterpart in the cycle of the Christian year, just because it points forward to that great, yet unfulfilled hope of the Church: the Ingathering of earth's nations to the Christ.[163]

Forgiveness

In this forgiveness of sins He presented His Person and authority as Divine, and He proved it such by the miracle of healing which immediately followed. Had the two been inverted, there would have been evidence, indeed, of His power, but not of his Divine Personality, nor of His having authority to forgive sins; and this, not the doing of miracles, was the object of His teaching and Mission, of which the miracles were only secondary evidence.[164]

It did not occur to [Peter] that the very act of numbering offenses marked an externalism which had never entered into, nor comprehended the spirit of Christ. Until seven times? Nay, until seventy times seven! Peter had yet to learn, what we, alas! Too often forget: that as Christ's forgiveness, so that of the Christian, must not be computed by numbers. It is *qualitative*, not *quantitative*: Christ forgives sin, not sins – and he who has experienced it, follows in His footsteps.[165]

God's forgiveness both cleans and cleanses; man's can do neither.[166]

---

163. LTJM, 582
164. LTJM, 349
165. LTJM, 560
166. Tohu, 10

Free Will

THE OLD TESTAMENT HAS settled, or rather anticipated, this great theological problem of so many ages: the combination and compatibility of God's sovereignty and decree with man's liberty and responsibility – not by either of our two clumsy devices or modes of cutting the knot – that from above in what is called Predestinarianism, or that from below in what is known as Arminianism – but by putting the two in juxtaposition.[167]

FOR THESE TWO ELEMENTS are always combined in a manner to us inexplicable, yet very really: the appointment of God and the free choice of man.[168]

I AM AFRAID I am not becoming more – what they call – orthodox; but I hope I am becoming more Christian. Formerly I used to find it much easier to be orthodox than now. I suppose I was working with thinner ropes. But now these two ropes – free grace and human responsibility – have grown so very large in my hands, that I am not strong enough to tie them together.[169]

Galilee

GALILEE WAS TO JUDAISM 'the Court of the Gentiles' – the Rabbinic Schools of Judea its innermost Sanctuary.[170]

EVEN THE HIGHLANDS OF Upper Galilee were not, like those of Judea, somber, lonely, enthusiasm-killing, but gloriously grand, free, fresh, and bracing. A more beautiful country – hill, dale, and lake – could scarcely be imagined than Galilee proper.[171]

---

167. Prophecy, 154
168. OT, 724
169. Tohu, 3
170. LTJM, 155
171. LTJM, 156

His Quotes

Genesis

THE BOOK OF GENESIS, and with it the first period of Covenant history, closes when the family had expanded into a nation. Finally with reference to the special arrangement of the "generations" recorded throughout the book of Genesis, it will be noticed that, so to speak, the side branches are always cut off before the main branch is carried onwards. Thus the history of Cain and of his race proceeds that of Seth and his race; the genealogy of Japheth and of Ham that of Shem; and the history of Ishmael and Esau that of Isaac and of Jacob. For the principle of election and selection, and of separation and of grace, underlies from the first the whole history of the covenant.[172]

Genesis 3:15

IN THE PROT-EVANGEL, AS Gen. 3:15 has been called, and in what follows it, we have as yet only the grand general outlines of the figure. Thus we see a *Person* in the Seed of the woman; *suffering*, in the prediction that His heel would be bruised; and *victory*, in that he would bruise the serpent's head. These merely general outlines are wonderfully filled up in the Book of Psalms.[173]

Gentiles

BUT, IT IS EXCEEDINGLY significant that Israel only is called "the first born." For this conveys that Israel was not to be alone in the family of God, but that, in accordance with the promise to Abraham, other sons should be born into the father's house. Thus even the highest promise spoken to Israel included in it the assurance of future blessings to the Gentiles.[174]

---

172. OT, 9
173. Temple, 91
174. OT, 170

If, as regards its content, the Book of Ruth stands on the threshold of the history of David, yet, as regards its spirit which the teaching of David breathes, do we love to remember that Israel's great king sprang from the union of Boaz and Ruth, which is symbolical of that between Israel and the Gentile world.[175]

In this sense, then, the Magi may truly be regarded as the representatives of the Gentile world; their homage as the first and typical acknowledgement of Christ by those who hitherto had been 'far off;' and their offerings symbolic of the world's tribute.[176]

Gideon

It was not from unbelief, nor yet in weakness of faith, that Gideon asked a sign from the Lord, or rather a token, a pledge of His presence. Those hours in the history of God's heroes, when, on the eve of a grand deed of the sublimest faith, the spirit wrestles with the flesh, are holy seasons, to which the superficial criticism of a glib profession, that has never borne the strain of utmost trial, cannot be applied without gross presumption.[177]

Gifts

Men's estimate of themselves is generally in the inverse ratio of their qualifications. How few, possessed of gifts, are willing to wait the call of God; how few even without gifts, or else who imagine they have gifts, are willing to wait![178]

---

175. OT, 391
176. LTJM, 149
177. OT, 362
178. Elisha, 6

His Quotes

As we use the gifts entrusted to us God will employ and increase them. Not to wait for more gifts or fresh opportunities, but to use what we have according to His direction, is the condition of increase.[179]

God

To make my refuge in God is the sum and substance of my faith.[180]

Oh what a God is our God, who has made the heavens the strings of His harp, and written His Name in the sky; the endless story in whose glory each day to its dying breath pours forth, and whose knowledge is nightly taught to a silent universe; whose sun, all-pervading in his gifts, is but the faint type of Him whose likeness of light he bears.[181]

For with God nothing is, in the real sense, future. "He seeth the end from the beginning."[182]

Next to the assurance of our salvation, the conviction most necessary to our comfort is that of God's continual Presence with us.[183]

The Being and Presence of God *is* the miraculous, and it *implies* the miraculous: For He is the Living and True God, and not merely Law or Force; but rather Force and Law are the outcome and the manifestation of God.[184]

What Jewish fathers and mothers were; what they felt towards their children; and with what reverence, affection, and care the latter returned what they had received, is known to every reader of the Old Testament. The relationship of father has its highest sanction and embodiment in

179. Elisha, 89
180. Golden, 47
181. Golden, 154
182. OT, 122
183. Elisha, 185
184. Elisha, xi

that of God towards Israel; the tenderness and care of a mother in that of the watchfulness and pity of the Lord over His people.[185]

For with God there is neither past nor future; neither immediate nor mediate; but all is one, the eternally and God-pervaded Present.[186]

By the Living and True God, I mean, not an abstraction, but a Person, a Moral Being; the Creator and owner of all; the Centre of all, with Whom all is living connection; or, in the words of St. Paul's quotation, He 'in whom we live and move and have our being.'[187]

'Jehovah reigneth' – these two words contain both the Law and the Gospel.[188]

Goliath

Pliny mentions an Arab giant who measured exactly the same as Goliath, and a man and a woman in the time of Augustus who were even an inch taller (Hist. Nat., 7.16). Josephus speaks of a Jew who was even taller (Ant., 18.4,5); and Keil refers to a giant of nearly the same proportions who visited Berlin in 1859.[189]

The Gospels

While thankfully retaining (I speak, of course, on my own part) what we hold to be intrinsically true and scientifically capable of ample defense – our belief in the Divine inspiration of the Gospels, we think of their writers, not as impersonal machines, but as inspired men, who in the preparation of their narratives availed themselves of the usual sources of historical composition, and whose writings (as regards their human

---

185. LTJM, 157
186. LTJM, 349
187. Prophecy, 118
188. Tohu, 1
189. OT, 469

aspect) are subject to all the ordinary canons of historical conclusion, we can address ourselves fearlessly, although with even more than usual reserve and caution, to the study of the literary origin of the Gospels, well assured that the results of the fullest historical investigation will establish the truth of Holy Scripture, and that anything that may seem to the contrary must be due to hasty inferences, or to insufficient consideration of both sides of the question, or else to want of such information, as, if we possessed it, would remove our difficulties.[190]

IF WE KEEP IN view the historical objection of St. Matthew, as primarily addressing himself to Jewish, while St. Luke wrote more especially for gentile readers, we arrive, at least, at one remarkable outcome of the variations in the narratives. Strange to say, the Judean Gospel gives the pro-Gentile, the gentile narrative the pro-Jewish, presentation of the event.[191]

IT IS IMPOSSIBLE TO read even a single page in the Gospels without being struck with the contrast between the spiritual tendency and direction of the Old Testament, as there brought to light, and the formalism and literalism of the Synagogue. A simple and impartial account of Judaism on the one hand, and a perusal of the Gospels on the other, constitutes one of the most convincing proofs of the Divine origin of the Christian religion, and of its organic connection with that of the Old Testament.[192]

IF A COPY OF the Gospels were put into the hands of an impartial Jewish historian, he could not fail to discover that the events there chronicled must have taken place exactly at the same time when, according to Christian belief, Jesus walked amongst men. The Gospels, historically speaking, cannot be an after-production.[193]

THAT THE WRITERS OF our Gospels should have so altered the original traditions and documents (which, according to our opponents, they elab-

---

190. Synoptic, 77
191. LTJM, 375
192. Nation, vii
193. Nation, viii

orated into their works), seems, to say the least, intellectually improbable, and morally absolutely incredible.[194]

THE OBSERVANT READER OF the New Testament will be struck by the peculiarity of the Old Testament quotations in the Gospels. As regards their form they are mostly neither exactly from the original Hebrew nor from the Septuagint. This in accordance with universal custom. For popular use the Scriptures were no longer quoted in the Hebrew, which was not spoken, nor from the LXX, which was under Rabbinic ban, but *targumed*, rendered into the vernacular; the principle being very strongly expressed that, in so doing, it was not the letter, but the meaning of the passage which was to be given.[195]

Gossip

IT IS A STRANGE manifestation of our love of the Church to be always speaking of her divisions and her weaknesses. If we really feel them, let us make it rather the subject of prayer than of talk.[196]

Grace

GRACE IS A DOCTRINE to be learned on my knees, to be understood on my knees, and to be applied on my knees.[197]

THE MEREST SPECK IN God's universe becomes a precious speck – a jewel – when God looketh upon it.[198]

THE WORD *IMPOSSIBLE* HAS no place in the vocabulary of grace; it only applies to me, not to Thee.[199]

   194. Prophecy, 67
   195. Prophecy, 117
   196. Elisha, 20
   197. Golden, 36
   198. Golden, 56
   199. Golden, 15

EXPERIENCE OF MUCH GRACE leads not to familiarity, but to holy awe; which is far different from slavish fear, in as much as it springs not from any apprehended consequences to ourselves, but from apprehension of His majesty and character.[200]

REMEMBER, GRACE IS GOD'S sufficiency in our insufficiency, God's rich giving in our abject poverty, God's coming in our tarrying, God's pouring forth in our emptiness.[201]

I KNOW NOT WHICH is more marvelous, the fullness or the unexpectedness of the provision which grace has made.[202]

THE PROMISES OF GRACE to those who walk in His ways are as numerous as they are necessary for our encouragement and comfort.[203]

FOR, FAITH IS INDEED an act, and *immediate*; and pardon also is an act, *immediate* and *complete*; but only the soul that has passed through it knows the terrible reality of a personal sense of sin, or the wondrous surprise of the sunrise of grace.[204]

WE REPEAT, IF WE take the words in their subjective aspect, as marking, not a new relation to God, but an inward state and condition: Regeneration means being begotten again, conversion means turning unto God. In such case, the one marks the Divine, the other the human aspect of the work of grace. In that view a man cannot be regenerated or begotten again of God, born from on high, without conversion or turning unto God; and, on the other hand, a man cannot be converted, or turn unto God, without having received the new nature, or being begotten of God and born again.[205]

---

200. Golden, 34
201. Golden, 43
202. Golden, 217
203. Golden, 228
204. OT, 541
205. Elisha, 168

Gratitude

Yet this "grace before meat," as we call it, is perhaps one of the truest tests of real devoutness. To take God's mercies without tacit, if not expressed acknowledgement or thanksgiving, is neither more nor less than profanity. It is simply heathenish. Worse than that, it is practically to disown the hand of the Lord, which alone can either give or bless the food.[206]

Greatness

He is great who is great in small things and on small occasions.[207]

Hate

Thus Saul's dark passions were ultimately concentrated in the one thought of murder. Yet in reality it was against Jehovah that he contended rather than against David. So true is it that all sin is ultimately against the Lord; so bitter is the root of self; and so terrible the power of evil in its constant growing strength, till it casts out all fear of God or care for man. So true also is it that "he that hateth his brother is a murderer," in heart and principle.[208]

Healing

I can scarcely find words strong enough to express my dissent from those who would limit Isa. 53:4, either on the one hand to spiritual, or on the other to physical 'sicknesses.' The promise is one of future deliverance from both, of a Restorer from all the woe which sin had brought.[209]

---

206. Name, 117
207. Tohu, 104
208. OT, 474
209. OT, 337

His Quotes

CHRIST HAS COME, AND is really the Healer of all disease and evil by being the Remover of its ultimate moral cause.[210]

Heart

THE HEART OF MAN is a many-stringed harp. One hand alone can sweep all its cords, and that is the hand which was nailed to the Cross.[211]

SHUT THE DOOR OF patience upon thy heart, lock it with the key of hope, and in faith hand its keeping over to Him Who is faithful.[212]

Heathenism

IN TRYING TO REALISE the views and feelings of heathenism under such circumstances [the Old Testament], we must beware of transporting into them our modern ideas. In our days the question is as to the acknowledgement or else the denial of Jehovah God. In those days it turned upon the acknowledgement or the opposite of Jehovah as the *only* true and living God, as this is expressed in the first commandment.[213]

Heaven

THE MORE CLOSELY WE view our heavenly inheritance, the more humbling and sad appear our low and carnal views concerning it.[214]

THERE MUST BE ABUNDANT employment and constant enjoyment there. And if such is the brightness of what we now see dimly, what must it be in the full light of His countenance?[215]

210. LTJM, 598
211. Tohu, 21
212. Tohu, 47
213. OT, 275
214. Golden, 117
215. Golden, 163

Sudden death is sudden glory to the children of God. One burst of light so bright, that all of earth fades in its glory; one mightier bound of life which, like the returning tide of strength in Samson, breaks down this temple; one louder blast which, like the trumpets of the priests, brings down the walls of the city; one mighty rush of joy, which carries before it the weak barriers – and all that we feared is passed. Our feet touch the other shore; we have not had the pang of parting, and we have the joy of meeting; we have not had the pain of death, and we have the joy of life; we have not heard the voice of weeping, and we are greeted by the songs of angels; we fell asleep on earth, and we woke up in heaven, in glory, with Christ, with all the saints.[216]

Besides, the utterances of the Old Testament on the subject of the 'hereafter' were, as became alike that stage of revelation and the understanding of those to whom it was addressed, far from clear. In the light of the New Testament it stands out in the sharpest proportions, although as an Alpine height afar off; but then that Light had not yet risen upon it.[217]

Taking the widest and most generous views of the Rabbis, they may be summed up: All Israel have share in the world to come; the pious among the Gentiles also have part in it. Only the perfectly just enter at once into paradise; all the rest pass through a period of purification and perfection, variously lasting, up to one year. But notorious breakers of the law, and especially apostates from the Jewish faith, and heretics, have no hope whatever, either here or hereafter! Such is the last word which the Synagogue has to say to mankind.[218]

Christ says: 'I am the door.' If the door is so glorious, what must be the building into which it opens![219]

---

216. Elisha, 214
217. LTJM, 748
218. Sketches, 165
219. Tohu, 14

His Quotes

Hebrew

IF GREEK WAS THE language of the court and camp, and indeed must have been understood and spoken by most in the land, the language of the people, spoken also by Christ and His disciples, was a dialect of the ancient Hebrew, the Western or Palestinian Aramaic. It seems strange, that this could ever have been doubted. A Jewish Messiah Who would urge His claim upon Israel in Greek, seems almost a contradiction in terms.[220]

AND HERE IT IS characteristic of Pharisaism, that Rabbinic Hebrew has not even a word equivalent to the term 'hypocrisy.'[221]

Higher Criticism

NOR LET US IMAGINE that the improvements upon the simplicity of the Gospel attempted by half-hearted believers, who trim their sails to catch every breeze of popularity, will ever lead to any result.[222]

SUCH WAS THE TEMPLE as restored by Herod – a work which occupied forty-six years to its completion. Yet, though the Rabbis never weary praising its splendour, not with one word do any of those who were contemporary indicate that its restoration was carried out by Herod the Great. So memorable an event in their history is passed over with the most absolute silence. What a complete answer does this afford to the objection sometimes raised from the silence of Josephus about the person and mission of Jesus.[223]

LET HIM NOT TAKE for granted that bold assertions of a negative character, made with the greatest confidence, even by men of undoubted learning and ability, are necessarily true. On the contrary, I venture to say, that

---

220. LTJM, 92
221. LTJM, 623
222. Golden, 184
223. Temple, 34

their trustworthiness is generally in inverse ration to the confidence with which they are made.[224]

THOSE MOST SUPERFICIALLY ACQUAINTED with modern theological controversy are aware, that certain opponents of the Bible have specially directed their attacks against the antiquity of the Pentateuch, although they have not yet arranged among themselves what parts of the Pentateuch were written by different authors, nor by how many, nor by whom, nor at what times, nor when or by whom they were ultimately collected into one book.[225]

FOR – TO TAKE the historical view of the question – even if every concession were made to negative criticism, sufficient would still be left in the Christian documents to establish a *consensus* of the earliest belief as to all the great facts of the Gospel-History, on which the preaching of the Apostles and the primitive Church have been historically based.[226]

FOR, THE MORE STRONGLY negative criticism asserts its position as to the Person of Jesus, the more unaccountable are His Teaching and the result of His Work.[227]

FOR, THE SOUND CRITIC should never devise an explanation for the sake of a supposed difficulty, but truthfully study the text – as an interpreter, not an apologist.[228]

FOR, IF THE LARGEST portions of the Old Testament are myths, legends, and forgeries, it would be difficult to retain any belief in the trustworthiness of the rest.[229]

---

224. OT, 405
225. Sketches, 186
226. LTJM, xiv
227. LTJM, 440
228. LTJM, 457
229. Prophecy, 213

His Quotes

To this may it be added, that in general the *argumentum ex silentio,* even if circumstances could not be otherwise satisfactorily explained, can never be satisfactory or convincing. It may raise doubts, but it cannot establish any facts. The non-observance of a law does not prove its non-existence.[230]

Hillel

We remember that, in his extreme old age and near his end, he may have presided over that meeting of Sanhedrin which, in answer to Herod's inquiry, pointed to Bethlehem as the birthplace of the Messiah (Matt. 2:4). We think of him also as the grandfather of that Gamaliel, at whose feet Saul of Tarsus sat. And to us he is the representative Jewish reformer, in the spirit of those times, and in the sense of restoring rather than removing.[231]

Of all persons mentioned in the literary and religious history of the Hebrew nation, few if any equal Hillel in fame.[232]

He also originated some changes in the management of theological schools, and was the first to introduce the distinctive titles of Rabban, Rabbi, and Rab (the latter being applied to extra-Palestinian teachers).[233]

Although the starting principles of these two teachers seem almost identical, their application and continual development would gradually bring to light and continually increase any real differences which obtained between them. Ultimately the differences became such, that it was said that, by the opposing teaching of Hillel and Shimmai, the one Torah had become two. Even during the lifetime of Hillel, great enmity prevailed between the rival schools, and, when on one occasion the parties accidentally met, blood was actually shed.[234]

230. Prophecy, 265
231. LTJM, 91
232. Nation, 133
233. Nation, 135
234. Nation, 139

AT LAST, AS MIGHT have been expected, compromise was found impossible. To settle the dispute, it was now asserted by the Hillelites that voice from Heaven (the Bat-Kol, literally daughter of the voice) had declared that the principles of both parties [Hillel and Shimmai] were the words of God, but that the Halacha, or traditional law, was to be fixed in accordance with the teaching of the school of Hillel.[235]

AS FREQUENTLY HAPPENS, WHERE offices, which depend on mental superiority, are connected with birth and station, the successors of Hillel had gradually increased in their pretensions, and equally declined in worth.[236]

History

IN ONE SENSE ALL history is Christian; for the government is on His shoulder. History either prepares the way *for* Christ or the way *of* Christ.[237]

FOR, SACRED HISTORY IS mainly the record of God's covenant-dealings. It chronicles events with the view of illustrating these dealings. Men and their actions are referred to only as far as needful to show what is the working of the Almighty.[238]

IN REAL LIFE THINGS do not move in precisely straight or rectangular lines, nor yet with the order and regulatory of a tale. Many and varied influences are always at work, and the theory which professes precisely to fit, and exactly to explain, all phenomena though they had to be constructed for that purpose, resembles rather the invention of a spectacular than the observed course of history.[239]

---

235. Nation, 161
236. Nation, 247
237. Golden, 61
238. Elisha, 12
239. Prophecy, 5

His Quotes

History has unfolded what the New Testament has infolded, and under the ever present guidance of the Holy Spirit we have learned to understand it.[240]

History, after the fall of the Roman Empire, recounts three periods: that of Authority, that of Inquiry, and that of Liberty. Of these, each (that has gone by) closed with a great war, and was characterized by some great reality that manifested its presence, by corresponding effects, in the political, intellectual, and religious life of the world. The age of authority, with its feudalism, scholasticism, and Popery, closed with the crusades; the age of inquiry with its king and state craft (its separate national life), its exhaustive study and lore, and its Reformation, closed with the French revolution. The third age is yet running, and from the liberty of nations evolves that of individuals; from the liberty of thought and inquiry, practical progress and social wellbeing; from its liberty of worship – in opposition to narrow-minded, scholastic dogmatism – the great reality of Christian Union.[241]

The Holy Land

It was the desire to preserve the nation and its learning in Palestine which inspired such sentiments as we are about to quote. "The air of Palestine makes one wise," said the rabbis . . . In the third and fourth centuries of our era they still taught, "He that dwelleth in Palestine is without sin."[242]

To put it more pictorially, the modern Palestine is about twice as large as Wales; it is smaller than Holland, and about equal in size to Belgium.[243]

Under ordinary circumstances, traveling in Palestine is no longer a dangerous undertaking. Still, the discomfort of having a bad instead of a serviceable horse, or of being exposed to the despotism of dragomans and

---

240. Prophecy, 112
241. Reformers, 215
242. Sketches, 5
243. Sketches, 8

the exactions of escorts are no trifling evils in a country where you have neither hotels, railways, nor telegraph.[244]

Holy Spirit

So true is it that all attempts at penitence, amendment, and religion, without the Holy Spirit of God and a change of heart, only tend to entangle man in the snare of self deception, to fill him with spiritual pride, and still further to increase his real alienation from God.[245]

Lastly, resistance to God must assuredly end in fearful judgment. Each conviction suppressed, each admonition stifled, each loving offer rejected, tends toward increasing spiritual insensibility, and that in which it ends. It is wisdom and safety to watch for the blessed influences of God's Spirit, and to throw open our hearts to the sunlight of His grace.[246]

As the Holy Spirit shines upon His own truth, the Scriptures are opened up to our spiritual understanding; holy desires drawn out faith, hope, and love quickened; and our prayers cease to be vague, and become special, and intensely earnest.[247]

Hosea 11:1

Those who have attentively followed the course of Jewish thinking, and marked how the ancient Synagogue, and that rightly, read the Old Testament in its unity, as ever pointing to the Messiah as the fulfillment of Israel's history, will not wonder at, but fully accord with St. Matthew's retrospective view [Matt 2:15]. The words of Hosea were in the highest sense 'fulfilled' in the flight to, and return of, the savior from Egypt.[248]

244. Athenaeum, 4/19/1859
245. Temple, 274
246. OT, 173
247. Golden, vii
248. LTJM, 150

His Quotes

Hospitality

True hospitality bestows its favors, not as giving, but rather as receiving favour. It is the hospitality of the heart, not of conventionalism, of pride, of selfishness, nor of what is called "society," which ever seeks back its own with tenfold interest.[249]

So far as the duty of hospitality is concerned, or the loving care for poor or sick, it were impossible to take a higher tone that that of Rabbanism. Thus it was declared, that "the entertainment of travelers was as great a matter as the reception of the *Shechinah*."[250]

Humility

Surely the greatest greatness of God is His condescension; His highest glory, His self-abasement![251]

But it is ever this humiliation of heart and simple faith in God's provision which are required for our healing.[252]

There are hours when it is manly to be unmanned – great to become little; hours, perhaps, in the religious life of those whose profession implies complete separation from the past – an act on which the soul risks its all, to which it devotes its affections, its energies, and inmost being – when a man must look back and reckon with himself, – when he must learn to look death in the face, and shake him familiarly by the hand. In the history of a man whose religion is a reality, nothing is small. His outward and real calmness has been the result of deep inward struggles; his serenity is the certitude of an inward and real victory.[253]

---

249. Elisha, 94
250. Sketches, 47
251. Golden, 264
252. OT, 782
253. Reformers, 229

Hypocrisy

So sometimes a word spoken even by ungodly men has served to awaken sinners, and to bring comfort to believers. But let us beware how we use religious phrases without realising their meaning. Few sins so harden the heart as hypocrisy; and among the causes which impoverish the soul, we place in the foremost rank the indiscriminate use of religious phraseology.[254]

Idolatry

Truly earth's gold is but dross, and its joys but toys.[255]

In the enjoyment of the creature let us learn how passing its beauty is, and how glorious and gracious the Creator.[256]

Idolatry is the religion of sight in opposition to that of faith.[257]

The worst of it was, that man gradually became conformed to his religion. He first imputed his own vices to his gods, and next imitated the vices of his god.[258]

Both strange nations and Israel itself, when in a state of apostasy, did not deny that Jehovah was God, but they tried to place Him on a level with other false deities. Now, Scripture teaches us that to place any other pretended God along with the living and true One argues as great ignorance, and is as great a sin, as to deny him entirely.[259]

---

254. Elisha, 313
255. Golden, 108
256. Golden, 155
257. OT, 46
258. OT, 46
259. OT, 91

His Quotes

IF OUR HEART CLEAVES to the world and its pleasures as our god, we are still of the world and in the world. But let us also remember that if our heart delights not in the Lord, if His ways are not pleasantness and peace, we still want the first element in genuine religion – a renewed heart.[260]

JEWS WERE TO AVOID passing through a city where there was an idolatrous feast – nay, they were not even to sit down within the shadow of a tree dedicated to idol-worship.[261]

ALL MEN ARE UNDER some influence. The question only is: what that influence is.[262]

Ignorance

THERE IS NO IGNORANCE so dangerous as experienced ignorance.[263]

Individuality

ALL OUR HUMANITY CENTRES in our individuality. All our virtue is the forthputting of individuality. All sin is the surrender of individuality.[264]

IT IS STRANGE HOW much more easily men are influenced in the mass than individually. Is it that the sense of danger and responsibility seems to decrease when it is shared by the many, or that spreading sympathy represses the influence of calculating thought?[265]

---

260. Elisha, 10
261. LTJM, 63
262. Tohu, 121
263. Tohu, 141
264. Tohu, 61
265. Elisha, 296

Influence

Nothing around us ever perisheth, it only lives in other forms; the flower, the leaf, the dust – all are imperishable. No movement ever wholly dies out. Every life, even the humblest, has its influences; some known, most unseen, and perhaps unfelt, but all real and lasting. And so we continue to live upon earth, and to speak, long after we have ceased to live, and our lips have been sealed in death. What solemn import does this give to every action, that its influence must for ever continue, not only as far as we, but so far as others also are concerned. In blessing or cursing, in brightness or in guilt, for God or for Satan, even the lowliest life endureth.[266]

Interpreting Scripture

For nothing could be more fatal to the proper understanding of Holy Scripture, or to the purpose of God in His dealings with His ancient people, than to transport into olden times the full spiritual privileges, the knowledge of Divine truth, or even that of right and duty, which we now enjoy. It is not to do honor, but dishonor, to the Spirit of God to overlook the educational process of gradual development, which is not only a necessity of our nature, but explains our history.[267]

The importance of a really serviceable dictionary of the Bible as an auxiliary in the study of the sacred text can hardly be overstated. To mention only one advantage, such a portable library of Biblical science saves an immense amount of labour, by presenting in a condensed form the results of the latest and most trustworthy investigations, while the student who may desire fuller information is at the same time directed to the sources whence it may best be derived.[268]

---

266. Elijah, 318
267. OT, 404
268. Athenaeum, 7/7/1860

His Quotes

Irreverence

FAMILIARITY HAS MADE MANY of us irreverent; not, indeed, that this familiarity is real, but imaginary. We imagine we know everything, though we see little beyond the reflection of our own narrow vision.[269]

Isaiah 6

EVEN WITHIN THE COMPASS of the Prophecies of Isaiah, there is no portion more sublime in its imagery, or solemn in its utterances, than the grand vision recorded in the sixth chapter. It is, so to speak, an Old Testament anticipation of the Book of Revelation.[270]

Isaiah 7:14

IT IS ONLY WHEN realizing this purpose of making a full end of the house of David, with all the Messianic promises and hopes bound up with it, that we fully understand how it evoked, in the case of Ahaz, that most full and personal Messianic prediction of "the Virgin's son."[271]

THE PROPHET'S COMMISSION TO Ahaz was threefold. He was to admonish him to courage (Isa. 7:4), and to announce that, so far from the purpose of the allies succeeding, Ephraim itself should, within a given time, cease to be "a people." Lastly, he was to give "a sign" of what had been said, especially of the continuance of the house of David. This was, in contrast to the king's unbelief, to point from the present to the future, and to indicate the ultimate object in view – the birth of the Virgin's Son, Whose name, Immanuel, symbolised all of present promise and future salvation connected with the house of David . . . This is not the place to attempt a detailed explanation – or rather vindication – of the Messianic prophecy, Isa. 7:14. We will only say that the intermingling of elements of the pres-

---

269. Elisha, 142
270. Tohu, 130
271. OT, 893

ent in the verses following the prophecy is, in our view, characteristic of all such prophecy.[272]

Isaiah 53

We do not wonder then at his question: Of Whom does the prophet speak? It is the same which in its ultimate idea, as the mystery of suffering, has engaged all thinking. Very really, it is the same which these eighteen centuries and more has divided us; which the Jew has sought to answer as he stood before the prophetic picture of Isaiah, and the Christian as he gazed on the crucified Christ.[273]

How perplexing it has proved to the Synagogue appears not only from the widely-divergent – rather absolutely contradictory – interpretations which the most learned of the Rabbis have given to this prophecy, but even from their own admission after they had attempted to solve its mystery.[274]

The prophecy speaks not only of suffering, but of conquering, and of conquering by suffering. Now suffering is human; conquering is divine: but to conquer by suffering is theanthropic.[275]

There is no fundamental divergence between Jew and Christian as regards the translation of this chapter. In this it differs from certain other passages designated as messianic, such as Genesis 49:10, Psalm 2:12, or the proper meaning of the word *almah* in Isaiah 7:14.[276]

---

272. OT, 896
273. Prophecy, 104
274. Prophecy, 104
275. Prophecy, 105
276. Prophecy, 106

His Quotes

TO THE ORTHODOX JEW, the fifty-third chapter of Isaiah is an inexplicable mystery; to the Reformed Jew, it is a hallucination; while to the Christian, it is a living reality.[277]

Islam

"PROPHET, HERO, SAGE, FANATIC, or imposter" – whatever theory we may adopt about Mohammed, the success of his mission constitutes a unique phenomenon in the history of the world. The rapid conquests of Islamism at first, and its continued sway for twelve centuries and over one hundred and eighty millions, form only part of the difficulty. In the birthplace of Christianity the Koran has taken the place of the Scriptures, and not only retained its hold on its professors, but offered effective resistance to the progress of European civilization ... It is a remarkable circumstance, that a creed apparently so simple, without mysteries, and with so few practical injunctions, should have given rise to more sects and heresies than perhaps any other religion.[278]

Israel

ISRAEL WAS "THE SON of God" by election, by grace, and by adoption.[279]

ISRAEL, AS A NATION, was not intended to attain pre-eminence either in art or science. If we may venture to pronounce on such matter, this was the part assigned, in the providence of God, to the gentile world. To Israel was specially entrusted the guardianship of the spiritual truth, which in the course of ages would develop in all its proportions, till finally it became the common property of the whole world.[280]

THE HISTORY OF ISRAEL and all their prospects were intertwined with their religion; so that it may be said that without their religion they had

277. Watchman, November 1877, p. 22
278. Athenaeum, 3/31/1860
279. OT, 170
280. OT, 591

no history, and without their history no religion. Thus, history, patriotism, religion, and hope alike pointed to Jerusalem and the Temple as the centre of Israel's unity.[281]

We must here call attention to the remarkable use of the term "Israel," not Judah, as applied to the southern kingdom, 2 Chron. 21:12, and also ver. 4. The same expression occurs in 2 Chron. 12:6; again in 15:17, and in 28:19, 27. In all these passages the name seems used with some reference to the law of God – as that which gave to Israel its name, and made it the people of Israel. It is almost an anticipation of the New Testament use of that name.[282]

In the Divine dispensation, Israel was destined to sustain the highest and most important part that can be assigned to any nation. Originally chosen to be the depository of spiritual truth, and separated from all other nations in order to fulfill this mission, it was preserved till the Divine purposes were accomplished. These purposes seem to have been, to serve as the channel, and as exemplification of Divine truth, and to afford a medium by which the fullness of Divine truth, and of Divine fact, might become embodied in the person of the Lord Jesus Christ.[283]

Israel, its history, its ordinances, its prophecies, all were not only so many present realities, they pointed also to something future, to which they stood in the relationship of shadows.[284]

Their past importance can scarcely be overstated; they gave to the world a Bible and a Saviour. Their present importance is indicated by their almost miraculous national preservation, and the fact of their being scattered by the Divine hand broad-cast over the fields of the world and of its history, as so many seeds of spiritual truths. Their future importance lies in this, that they are seeds which are yet to take root, to spring up and

---

281. LTJM, 3
282. OT, 806
283. Nation, 1
284. Nation, 2

His Quotes

to bear fruit; and that their future is connected with the last and brightest events of coming history.[285]

ISRAEL AND ITS HISTORY are inseparably connected with Scripture.[286]

ISRAEL CAN BE NEITHER transformed nor subdued by the hand of man. They belong to God.[287]

WHEN ISRAEL WENT INTO Babylon, it was once more like going into Egypt. The return to Palestine was another Exodus. But, oh, how different from the first! That had been marked by the glowing religion of the Old Testament; this, by what we know as Judaism. Israel returned from the Exile not as Israel, but as the Jews; such as history has ever since presented them.[288]

THERE ARE FOUR WONDERFUL things about Israel: their election, their rejection, their unbelief, and their ingathering.[289]

ISRAEL'S FIRST SIN WAS in asking, their last in rejecting, a king[290].

Jacob

THE CONTEST WITH ESAU was nothing; the contest with Jehovah everything. The Lord could not be on Jacob's side, till he had been disabled, and learned to use other weapons than those of his own wrestling. Then it was that Jacob recognized with whom he had hitherto wrestled.[291]

285. Nation, 5
286. Nation, 5
287. Nation, 27
288. Prophecy, 300
289. Tohu, 7
290. Tohu, 7
291. OT, 96

Never, after that night, did Jacob again contend with carnal weapons; and though the old name of Jacob reappears again and again by the side of his new designation, it was to remind both him and us that Jacob, though halting, is not dead, and that there is in us always the twofold nature, alike Jacob and of Israel.[292]

Such was the end of Jacob – the most pilgrim-like of the pilgrim fathers.[293]

James

The task of directing and governing the Jewish section of the infant Church could not have been entrusted to one better suited for the trying duty than the apostle James. Gifts and graces, birth and education, habits and sympathies, natural character and spiritual qualifications, equally fitted him for it. He had all Peter's amiableness and ready to yield, the result of a gushing nature, without any of his weakness; all Paul's unswerving decidedness, without any of his occasional sternness; all Phillip's spirit of inquiry, without either the skepticism of Thomas, or the spiritual unimpressionableness of Philip himself; all John's intensity, without any of the somewhat dangerous tendency of such natures toward enthusiasm.[294]

He yielded to the Jews and he yielded to the Gentiles; he counseled the decrees of Jerusalem and he counseled Paul's Nazarite Vow; he bent towards the one and he bent towards the other, but only that he might thereby unite them together in Christ.[295]

James was, in the first place, a *Jewish believer*; in the second place, he was an *Apostle of Jesus Christ*; lastly, he was *an Apostle for and to the circumcision*.[296]

292. OT, 96
293. OT, 130
294. Scattered Nation, January 1868
295. Scattered Nation, January 1868
296. Scattered Nation, July 1868

His Quotes

Jericho

Pilgrims, priests, traders, robbers, anchorites, wild fanatics, such were the figures to be met on that strange scene; and almost within hearing were the sacred sounds from the Temple-mount in the distance . . . According to the Jerus. Talmud (succ. v 3) six different acts of ministry in the Temple were heard as far as Jericho, and the smell of the burning incense also could be perceived there.[297]

It is the Eden of Palestine, the very fairyland of the old world. And how strangely is the gem set! Deep down in the hollowed valley, through which tortuous Jordan winds, to lose his waters in the slimy mass of the Sea of Judgment.[298]

Jerusalem

Yet Jerusalem was almost marked out by nature to be Israel's capitol, from its strength, its central position, and its situation between Benjamin and Judah. Far more than this, it was the place of which the Lord had made choice; to be, as it were, a guarded sanctuary within the holy land.[299]

"Ten measures of beauty," say the Rabbis, "hath God bestowed upon the world, and nine of these fall to the lot of Jerusalem" – and again, "A city, the fame of which has gone out from one end of the world to the other." . . . in opposition to her rival Alexandria, which was designated "the little," Jerusalem was called "the great." It almost reminds one of the title 'eternal city,' given to Rome, when we find the rabbis speaking of Jerusalem as the "eternal house." Similarly, if a common proverb has it, that "all roads lead to Rome," it was a Jewish saying, "All coins come from Jerusalem."[300]

297. Sketches, 63
298. LTJM, 716
299. OT, 522
300. Sketches, 79

It was the temple which gave character to Jerusalem, and which decided its fate.[301]

I envy not the man who can gaze for the first time upon the battlemented walls, the domes, the fantastic minarets, and the terraced roofs of the sacred city of Jerusalem without emotion. How numerous are the associations connected with that Holy City; how solemn are its memories; and how awful, in the fulfillment of every detail foretold, has been its fate![302]

In every age, the memory of Jerusalem has stirred the deepest feelings. Jews, Christians, and Mohammedans turn to it with reverent affection. It almost seems as if in some sense each could call it his 'happy home,' the 'name ever dear' to him. For our holiest thoughts of the past, and our happiest hopes for the future, connect themselves with 'the city of our God.'[303]

In all his wanderings the Jew had not seen a city like his own Jerusalem. Not Antioch in Asia, not even imperial Rome herself, excelled it in architectural splendour. Nor has there been, either in ancient or modern times, a sacred building equal to the Temple, whether for situation or magnificence; nor yet have there been festive throngs like those joyous hundreds of thousands who, with their hymns of praise, crowded towards the city on the eve of Passover.[304]

Assuredly, when the Rabbis thought of their city in her glory, they might well say: 'The world is like unto an eye. The ocean surrounding the world is the white of the eye; its black is the world itself; the pupil is Jerusalem, but the image within the pupil is the sanctuary.[305]

---

301. Sketches, 82
302. Modern, 43
303. Temple, 1
304. Temple, 6
305. Temple, 16

His Quotes

SILENCE HAS FALLEN THESE many centuries upon Israel; but the very stones of Jerusalem's ruin and desolation have cried out that He, Whom in their silence they rejected, has come as King in the Name of the Lord.[306]

THE CITY FORMS A sort of irregular quadrangle, and yet, from another point of view, the Temple mount seems so situated that the whole city appears to lie in a semi-circle around, as it were to guard it. In circumference, the city may extend about four miles. But its great peculiarity lies in its situation and structure. Imagine yourself then on the boundary line between Benjamin and Judah. This is the spot on which Jerusalem is built. Indeed, our teachers contend that the line which separated the two tribes should be drawn through the very court of the Temple.[307]

Jesus

ALL THAT HE IS, He is for us.[308]

EACH OF CHRIST'S TITLES seems one of the pearly gates through which blessed and unlimited views of heaven open.[309]

NO PROPHET OF THE Lord ever had or claimed power, like the magicians; but in every case the gracious influence was specially, and for that time, transmitted directly from God. Only the God-Man had power in Himself, so that His every contact brought health and life.[310]

OF COURSE, HIS WAS a pious Jewish home ... His mind was so thoroughly imbued with the sacred Scriptures – He was familiar with them in every detail – that we cannot fail to infer that the home of Nazareth possessed a

---

306. LTJM, 729
307. Scattered, 1869, Grey to Dawn, ch. 9
308. Golden, 280
309. Golden, 288
310. OT, 277

precious copy of its own of the entire Sacred Volume, which from earliest childhood formed, so to speak, the meat and drink of the God-man.[311]

HAD HE ENTIRELY DISCARDED the period in which He lived, had He not availed Himself of all in it that was true or might be useful, he would not have been of it – not the true man Christ Jesus. Had He followed it, identified himself with its views and hopes, or headed its movements, he would not have been the Christ, the Son of the living God, the promised Deliverer from sin and guilt.[312]

JESUS SPOKE AS TRULY a Jew to the Jews, but He spoke not as they – no, not as their highest and best Teachers would have spoken. And this contrariety of spirit with manifest similarity in form is, to my mind, one of the strongest evidences of the claims of Christ, since it raises the all important question, whence the teacher of Nazareth – or, shall we say, the humble child of the carpenter-home in a far-off little place of Galilee – had drawn His inspiration.[313]

IF THE CLAIMS OF Jesus have been rejected by the Jewish Nation, he has at least, undoubtedly, fulfilled one part of the Mission prophetically assigned to the Messiah . . . Passing the narrow bounds of obscure Judea, and breaking down the walls of national prejudice and isolation, He has made the sublimer teaching of the Old Testament the common possession of the world, and founded a great Brotherhood, of which the God of Israel is the father.[314]

THE MAN OF NAZARETH has, by universal consent, been the mightiest Factor in our world's history: alike politically, socially, intellectually, and morally. If He be not the Messiah, He has at least thus far done the Messiah's work. If He be not the Messiah, the world has not, and never can have, a Messiah.[315]

311. Sketches, 111
312. Sketches, 267
313. LTJM, xii
314. LTJM, 127
315. LTJM, 127

His Quotes

He was what Israel was intended to have become to mankind; what it was the final object of Israel to have been. In Him was God's gift to mankind.[316]

If the teaching of Christ was new and was true, so must His work have been. And in this lies the highest vindication of this miracle, - that He is the miracle.[317]

And yet, was it not after all true – that he was either the Christ - the Son of God, or a blasphemer?[318]

When he is most human (in the moment of His being nailed to the Cross), then He is most Divine, in the utter discarding of the elements of human instrumentality and of human suffering.[319]

In one sense Jesus Christ certainly was a man of his time: He spoke the language of His time, and he addressed Himself by word and deed to the men, the ideas, and the circumstances of His time . . . . But in another and higher sense Jesus Christ was not the man of His time, spake not, acted not, aimed not, as they: and hence the great body of the people rejected, denounced, and crucified, while even His own so often misunderstood and were surprised by Him.[320]

In this respect, also, it is characteristic that the name 'Son of David' was the most distinctive title claimed by, and given to Jesus, while in the case of all spurious messianic movements this occupied only a subordinate, if any, place.[321]

---

316. LTJM, 284
317. LTJM, 380
318. LTJM, 861
319. LTJM, 882
320. Prophecy, 13
321. Prophecy, 18

Jesus' Teaching

His Presence, that one grand presence is, indeed, ever the same. But God always adapts His teaching to our learning; else it were not teaching at all, least of all Divine teaching.[322]

There was no appeal to human authority, other than that of the conscience; no subtle logical distinctions, legal niceties, nor clever sayings. Clear, limpid, and crystalline, flowed His words from out the spring of the Divine Life that was in Him.[323]

He who taught such new and strange truth could never be called a mere reformer of Judaism. There cannot be 'reform,' where all the fundamental principles are different.[324]

Once more we notice, how in Deeds, as in His words, the Lord adopted forms known and used by His contemporaries, while He filled them with quite other substance.[325]

In all His teaching, except when in the Synagogue of Nazareth He pointed to His message of the kingdom as fulfilling the prophecy of Isaiah, He did not base His Messianic claims on any special prophecies.[326]

Suppose you even proved that much in His sayings found a counterpart in Rabbinical authorities – what then? In the one case you have a little gold with much dross; in the other, pure gold without any dross. Whence the difference?[327]

---

322. LTJM, 263
323. LTJM, 331
324. LTJM, 380
325. LTJM, 599
326. Prophecy, 115
327. Tohu, 13

His Quotes

Jewish Evangelism

No one who takes the word of God as his guide can for a moment question that our Blessed Lord has laid upon His Church a special duty in regard to Israel. If, in the abstract it is true, that a Church which is not aggressive or missionary has lost her convictions, her life, her very *raison d'etre*, this applies with tenfold force to work among Israel. The very parting commission which our Lord left his Church, so to speak, as the outcome, the heritage, and the fellowship of His own work on earth, contained this special direction, good for all ages: "beginning at Jerusalem."[328]

We believe two duties here devolve upon us: to wake the Church to a scriptural and spiritual view of her relation to Israel, and to make known the glorious gospel to our Jewish brethren, by lifting up a testimony for Christ in every land, that so "the remnant" may be called out and saved, and preparation made for a greater and wider work, which, although apparently unconnected with our present missions, is none the less the direct outcome of them.[329]

We are not in the least disturbed by the persistent clamour of our brethren in the Synagogue, that the conversion of the Jews is an impossibility, and every Jewish convert either an ignorant dupe or a cunning hypocrite.[330]

By far wider results have been obtained by Jewish missions than the ingathering of even thousands of Jewish believers. Judaism itself has been affected. In every place the presence of the Jewish missionary has of itself had the effect of calling attention to Christianity.[331]

---

328. Watchman, June, 1877, p. 85
329. Watchman, June, 1877, p. 86
330. Watchman, June 1877, p. 86
331. Watchman, June 1877, p. 87

Jewish History

DURING THE EIGHTEEN CENTURIES of their dispersion God has, so to speak, forced the land and the people upon universal notice. He has scattered the people among all nations, but not suffered them to mingle with any; He has allowed then to be persecuted, but not destroyed. At this moment, in spite of strong counter-currents, the Jews are as distinct and separate as they were at any previous period in their history; despite the leveling influences of civilisation and trade, they stand out as probably the most prominent, intellectually and financially, in every country of Europe.[332]

YET WE VENTURE TO assert that a more vigorous intellectual life can scarcely be conceived than that of the Jews, not only during the golden period of their comparative prosperity, but even during the darkest ages of persecution.[333]

IT IS MY DELIBERATE conviction that Jewish history casts much light on the evangelical accounts in the Gospels, on the book of Acts, and the later Ecclesiastical History, both in its records of the spread of Christianity, and the origin and development of heretical sects.[334]

AS THEIR PAST HISTORY, so their presence continuance is a mystery, which we firmly believe can only be solved by a reference to their future destiny. Even in their dispersion the prophetic utterances concerning them still holds true: "Lo, the people shall dwell alone, and shall not be reckoned among the nations."[335]

FROM THE VERY TIME when the prophecy of Moses began to be fulfilled, that the Jew was to become "an astonishment, a proverb, and a byword among all nations, wither the Lord shall lead thee," to within the last hundred years, Jewish history has been one of bitter persecution and oppres-

---

332. Watchman, March 1877, p. 4
333. Athenaeum, 12/19/1887
334. Nation, vii
335. Peculiar, p. 319

sion. And yet how cruelly alike have been the sufferings inflicted upon the Jew by his various tyrannical masters! What a monotony there is in the record of his calamities, – calamities by which other nations would have been swept away, and yet the Jew remains! The existence of the race of Israel and the truth of the inspired Scriptures go hand in hand. Until men tear out of human history every page brightened with Jewish glory and watered with Jewish tears, they never can shake the infallible authority of the Word, or lesson the deep foundation of our historical Christianity.[336]

WHAT AN ANOMALY TO the history of mankind is the Jew! Mingling with the various nations among whom he has been scattered, his national character has never been lost. He belongs, and always will belong, to a peculiar and distinct people. He is a burning lamp kept alive amid convulsions and tempests – a subject without a king, having survived oppression in every form; while his conquerors are dead, and empires, which bound him in the chains of tyranny, have perished forever.[337]

IT HAS OFTEN BEEN asked by those who dispute the claims of the Hebrew race to be regarded as a highly intellectual people, why the Jews have never produced great poets, great orators, or great writers? To this question Mr. Disraeli answers: "Favored by Nature and by Nature's God, we produced the lyre of David; we gave you Isaiah and Ezekiel: they are our 'Olynthians,' our 'Phillippies.' Favored by Nature we still remain but in exact proportion as we have been favored by nature, we have been persecuted by man. After a thousand struggles; after acts of heroic courage that Rome has never equaled; deeds of patriotism that Athens and Sparta and Carthage have never excelled; we have endured fifteen hundred years of supernatural slavery during which every device that can degrade or destroy man has been the destiny that we have sustained and baffled. . . . And as for great writers, the catalogue is not blank. What are all the schoolmen, Aquinas himself, to Maimonides? And as for modern philosophy, all springs from Spinoza."[338]

---

336. Modern, 18
337. Modern, 129
338. Modern, 171

The Wisdom of Alfred Edersheim

Jewish Views of Jewish Believers in Jesus

"They have left their father's home and their mother's bosom, to join the enemy and the cruel scoffer. They are strangers now; they have another God, another people, other laws, other worship, other language, other manners, other pursuits. And yet they can never be strangers; they are ours – flesh of our flesh, bone of our bone. They are dead; mourned as such, put away as such. And yet they are living. You speak of the dead, you think of them, you love them, you picture them as in glory, as perfect, and you hope soon to rejoin them. But though you have bewailed the apostate as dead, you may not think of them, nor love them, nor hope to join them, nor associate their memory with God and with good. The apostate is dead, in the sense of all that is repugnant in death."[339]

For the most unrelenting persecution follows the Jews on whom the faintest suspicion of apostasy rests. His character, his conduct, and his motives are impugned; the vilest dishonesty, the most base degradation of what is highest and holy are freely charged against him. A man may live worse than a careless, an immoral life, and they will condone it; he may doubt almost every distinctive doctrine of Judaism, even its fundamental principles, and they will only shrug their shoulders. But conversion to Christianity, in the sense of belief, is deemed absolutely impossible, and is unpardonable.[340]

The supposed apostate was to be crushed, hunted down like vermin, and destroyed, and that by persons who themselves cared not a whit for Judaism, only that they were born in its communion, and would not allow anyone to forsake it.[341]

---

339. Rosenbaum, 21
340. Rosenbaum, 32
341. Name, 67

His Quotes

Jezebel

THE CLASSICAL STUDENT WILL be interested to know that Jezebel was the grand-aunt of Dido, the founder of Carthage.[342]

JEZEBEL POSSESSED, IN NO small measure, the fanaticism, the firmness, and the fierceness, for which her race was famous in history.[343]

Job

TWO THINGS MAY BE regarded as quite settled about the book of Job. Its scene and actors are laid in patriarchal times, and outside the family or immediate ancestry of Abraham. It is a story of a gentile life in the time of the earliest patriarchs. And yet anything more noble, grand, devout, or spiritual than what the book of Job contains is not found, 'no, not in Israel.'[344]

John's Gospel

THE SCENE WHICH FOLLOWED [John 7:46–52] is so thoroughly Jewish, that it alone would suffice to prove the Jewish, and hence Johannine, authorship of the Fourth Gospel.[345]

John the Baptist

WHAT WAS DISTINCTIVE IN the words of the Baptist, seems his view of *sin* as a totality, rather than sins: implying the removal of that great barrier

---

342. OT, 663
343. Elisha, 2
344. OT, 47
345. LTJM, 586

between God and man, and the triumph in that great contest indicated in Gen. 3:15, which Israel after the flesh failed to perceive.[346]

AND NOW, OF A SUDDEN, 'the Voice' was heard in the wilderness! It was not that of Pharisee, Sadducee, Essene, or Nationalist – and yet the Baptist combined the best elements of all these directions.[347]

THAT HE WAS SIMPLE, absolutely self-surrendering, and trustful, almost as a child, every act of his life testifies.[348]

IF – WITH REVERENCE be it said – the mission of Jesus Christ might be summed up in these words, 'Our Father which art in heaven,' that of His forerunner is contained in these: Lo, the kingdom of God, promised of old to our fathers![349]

Jonathan

WHATEVER FITNESS HE MIGHT have shown for "the kingdom," had he been called to it, a more unselfish, warm-hearted, genuine, or noble character is not presented to us in Scripture than that of Jonathan.[350]

Joseph

ON THE OTHER HAND, Joseph seems to have united some of the best characteristics of his ancestors. Like Abraham, he was strong, decided, and prudent; like Isaac, patient and gentle; like Jacob, warmhearted and affectionate. Best of all, his conduct signally differed from that of his brethren. On the other hand, however, it is not difficult to perceive how even the promising qualities of his natural disposition might become sources of

346. LTJM, 238
347. Prophecy, 354
348. Prophecy, 356
349. Prophecy, 366
350. OT, 453

moral danger. Of this the history of Joseph's ancestors had afforded only too painful evidence.[351]

Josephus

Besides, however untruthful Josephus was, he may, as a general rule, be trusted where official numbers, capable of verification, are concerned.[352]

Josephus always carefully suppresses, so far as possible, all that refers to the Christ – probably not only in accordance with his own religious views, but because mention of a Christ might have been dangerous, certainly would have been inconvenient, in a work written for readers in Rome.[353]

If Josephus was not from the first a traitor, his *conduct*, at least, appears sufficiently treasonable, and seems to have early roused the suspicion of his colleagues . . . From the moment he betrayed his country's cause, he was as violently hated and persecuted as he had been respected by the Jews.[354]

He was truly an eclectic Jew. The Pharisees, the Sadducees, the Essenes, and the Grecians, might equally claim him by turns.[355]

His systematic ignoring of Christianity will scarcely seem strange when we remember the character of the man, the ulterior object of his writings, and the relations between Christianity and Judaism, on the one hand, and heathenism, on the other.[356]

351. OT, 101
352. Temple, 8
353. LTJM, 150
354. Nation, 34
355. Nation, 37
356. Prophecy, 87

Joshua

And so it was only after many years that Oshea became Joshua, while the name Joshua was given to our Lord by the angels before his birth (Matt 1:21). The first *became*, the second *was* Joshua. And so the name and the work of Joshua pointed forward to the fullness in Christ, alike by what it was and by what it was not, and this in entire accordance with the whole character and object of the Old Testament.[357]

Joy

The rule for securing permanent happiness is to delight ourselves in the law of Jehovah – in the twofold sense of having this as our spiritual object and cherishing a spiritual apprehension of it.[358]

Our joy lies not merely in what we have escaped from, but in what we have obtained; not merely in what has been taken from us, but in what has been given to us.[359]

Judea

True, its landscapes were comparatively barren, its hills bare and rocky, its wilderness lonely; but around those grey limestone mountains gathered the sacred history – one might almost say, the romance and religion of Israel.[360]

---

357. OT, 339
358. Golden, 4
359. Golden, 118
360. Sketches, 58

His Quotes

Judah HaNasi

JUDAH'S EMINENT PIETY, MODESTY, and learning, secured not only the universal respect of his contemporaries, but attached to his name the title "Ha-Kadosh," the holy, and surrounded him in the synagogue with a halo of almost super-human glory.[361]

Judaism

ON THE QUESTION OF what are the real principles of Judaism, a fundamental divergence exists at the very outset. We all know that, roughly speaking, Judaism is ranged into two parties, Orthodox and Reformed, and that the former rests its interpretation of the Old Testament on the laws and principles of the Talmud, while the latter has embarked on that boundless sea which leads – to nowhere, the difference between the various shades of opinion being marked by a nearer or farther distance from the shore.[362]

AN EXTRA-PALESTINIAN JUDAISM, WITHOUT priesthood, altar, temple, sacrifices, tithes, first-fruits, Sabbatical and Jubilee years, must first set aside the Pentateuch, unless, as in Christianity, all these be regarded as blossoms designed to ripen into fruit, as types pointing to, and fulfilled in higher realities.[363]

Judas Iscariot

THE BETRAYER ALONE WAS too busy with his plans to finish the meal. He had, so to speak, separated from the fellowship of Israel before he excommunicated himself from the Church.[364]

---

361. Nation, 504
362. Watchman, July 1877, p. 115
363. Sketches, 4
364. Temple, 200

DID CHRIST KNOW FROM the beginning that Judas would betray him, and yet, so knowing, did He choose him to be one of the Twelve? Here we can only answer by indicating this as a canon in studying the life on Earth of the God-man, that it was part of His [emptying of Himself], and taking upon himself the form of a servant (Phil 2:7), voluntarily to forego His Divine knowledge in the choice of His human actions.[365]

Judges

THE JUDGES WERE ISRAEL'S *representative men* – representatives of its faith and its hope, but also of its sin and decay.[366]

AND THUS THE PERIOD of the judges ends as every other period. It contains the germ of, and points to something better; but it is imperfect, incomplete, and fails, though even in its failure it points forward. Judges must be succeeded by kings, and kings by *the* king – the true Nazarite, the Lord Jesus Christ.[367]

Judgment

THE ULTIMATE DESTRUCTION OF sinners is not an act of vengeance; it is the necessary manifestation of the character of Jehovah.[368]

THERE IS A RIPENING either for Heaven or for Hell, presently going on in the case of everyone.[369]

Far more frequently are folly and sin punished in the ordinary course of Providence than by special judgments.[370]

---

365. LTJM, 822
366. OT, 342
367. OT, 343
368. Golden, 51
369. Elisha, 13
370. LTJM, 655

His Quotes

AND HERE WE MARK, that there is always terrible literality about the prophecies of judgment, while those of blessing far exceed the words of prediction.[371]

SO HAS IT EVER been: the rod of His vengeance, after having served its purpose, has always been speedily broken into pieces.[372]

Kaparot[373]

AS THE JEWS HAVE no High Priest, and no altar, they endeavor to keep up the spirit of the law by this self-devised sacrifice. Nothing can be clearer proof of the deeply-rooted conviction in the heart of the Hebrew that without the shedding blood there is no remission of sins. Had the Rabbis really believed that repentance, or the Day of Atonement itself, or alms-giving and the like, really atoned for sin, they would never have devised such a custom as this.[374]

Kingdom of God

SACRED HISTORY IS PRIMARILY that of the kingdom of God, and only secondarily that of individuals and periods.[375]

THREE IDEAS ESPECIALLY DID this Kingdom of God imply: *universality, heavenliness, and permanency.*[376]

---

371. LTJM, 803
372. Nation, 47
373. (This is a custom on the Day of Atonement. A live chicken is cut with a knife, the blood is poured out, and the chicken is waved above the head of the person holding it. The chicken's blood is seen as a substitution for the person.)
374. Modern, 103
375. OT, 341
376. LTJM, 184

'THE KINGDOM OF GOD,' or Kingly Rule of God, is an *objective fact*. The visible Church can only be the *subjective* attempt at its outward realization, of which the invisible Church is the true counterpart.[377]

CHRIST CAME TO FOUND a Kingdom, not a school; to institute a fellowship, not to propound a system.[378]

AND THE LESSON TO us is, that, just as the Old Testament gives neither the national history of Israel, nor the biography of its heroes, but a history of the Kingdom of God in its progressive development, so the Gospels present not a 'Life of Christ,' but the history of the Kingdom of God in its progressive manifestation.[379]

THE NARROW BOUNDARIES OF Judah and Israel were to be enlarged so as to embrace all men, and one King would reign in righteousness over a ransomed world that would offer to Him its homage of praise and service. All that had marred the moral harmony of earth would be removed; the universal fatherhood of God would become the birthright of redeemed, pardoned, regenerated humanity; and all this blessing would centre in, and flow from, the Person of the Messiah.[380]

THUS THE OLD TESTAMENT pointed beyond itself to the perfectness which it announced and for which it prepared. That perfectness consists in the removal of all the evil which sin has wrought, in the restoration of man to God, and in the fullness of blessings which flows from fellowship between God and man. This is the Kingdom of God.[381]

---

377. LTJM, 186
378. LTJM, 365
379. LTJM, 393
380. Prophecy, 24
381. Prophecy, 139

His Quotes

Law of Moses

THERE IS, AS DIVINES express it, a threefold use of the law: as schoolmaster to Christ, to hedge up sinners and prevent them from gross iniquity; next, what is designated as its principal and primary object, to teach believers more fully, day by day, what is the will of their Father; and, lastly, to admonish them to walk therein.[382]

WHEN MOST LEGAL WE were greatest law-breakers; when most free from the law we were its closest observers.[383]

YET HOW OFTEN AND grievously have we misunderstood the import of the law, while we were under its domain! Then it spoke only of us, now it speaks only of Him.[384]

THREE GREAT OBSERVANCES HERE stand out prominently. Around them the faith and the worship alike of the ancient patriarchs, and afterwards of Israel may be said to have clustered. They are: *circumcision, sacrifices* and the *Sabbath*.[385]

AGAIN, ALMOST ALL THE commands are put in a *negative* form ("thou shalt not"), implying that transgression, not obedience, is natural to us.[386]

SUCH LAW WAS NEVER given by man; never dreamed of in his highest conceptions. Had man only been able to observe it, assuredly not only life hereafter but happiness and joy here would have come with it. As it were, it brought only knowledge of sin.[387]

382. Golden, 159
383. Golden, 159
384. Golden, 160
385. OT, 152
386. OT, 206
387. OT, 207

ISRAEL WAS GOD'S OWN possession. Before hallowing and formally setting it apart, God marked it out, and drew the boundary-lines around His property. Such was the object and the meaning of the ordinances (Exod. 20:22–23:33), which preceded the formal conclusion of the covenant, recorded in Exodus 24.[388]

ALIKE THE LAWS, THE worship, the institutions, and the mission of Israel were intended to express these two things; acknowledgement of God and dependence upon God.[389]

As [PAUL] EXPLAINS IT, the Law could not reach within, and, therefore, did not remove, rather did it call out, that sin on which it pronounced the sentence of death. Accordingly, the object of the Law could only have been to call forth longing after salvation. It follows, that the Law could only have been intended as a temporary institution and to be a schoolmaster unto Christ.[390]

IN GENERAL WE MUST repeat, that the religious institutions of Israel were adapted not to what Israel then was, but rather to what Israel was intended to become. If Israel had developed in the right direction, if it had come up to its institutions, then – but only then – would these institutions have been possible, and have become a practical reality.[391]

FOR, AFTER ALL, THE Law is not the final object, but only means for attaining it (I mean, the Law in its positive, not its negative aspect, the 'thou shalt,' not the 'thou shalt not'). The final object is holiness and growth unto God.[392]

BUT A LAW, WHICH is to be observed only so far as convenient, is no law at all.[393]

388. OT, 208
389. Prophecy, 45
390. Prophecy, 182
391. Prophecy, 240
392. Tohu, 84
393. Watchman, July 1877, p. 115

His Quotes

Legalism

CEREMONIALISM RAPIDLY DEVELOPS, TOO often in proportion to the absence of spiritual life.[394]

PEOPLE WHO ARE VERY particular about secondary matters are never very earnest about primary. The greatest prude is not generally the most modest woman. I distrust the generalship of the soldier who is a martinet, and I doubt the reality of those theologians who are so rabid about smaller points.[395]

OUR CHURCHISM IS MOSTLY like withered leaves – showing where life has been.[396]

MUCH THAT PASSES FOR evangelical teaching is like brushing a napless coat. You may make it shiny, but you only show the more clearly that there is no wool on the cloth.[397]

Leviticus

PERHAPS WE MIGHT GO so far as to say, that part 1 of Leviticus exhibits, in symbolical form, the doctrine of *justification,* and part 2 that of *sanctification;* or, more accurately: the manner of *access to God*, and the *holiness* which is the result of that access.[398]

WE REPEAT IT: THE Book of Leviticus is intended for Israel as the people of God; it is the statute-book of Israel's spiritual life; and, on both these grounds, it is neither simply legal, in the sense of ordinary law, nor yet

---

394. LTJM, 814
395. Tohu, 5
396. Tohu, 9
397. Tohu, 30
398. OT, 224

merely ceremonial, but throughout *symbolical and typical.* Accordingly, its deeper truths apply to all times and to all men.[399]

Life

For, as time is made up of moments, so life mostly of small actions whose greatness lies in their combination.[400]

It is as when we look down into the deep blue sea, or up into the deep blue sky. Examined separately, each particle of that water, or of that air, seems colourless. Only when viewed in its totality do we become aware of its shadings. So is life. Each action separately may have its excuse, its reasonable motive, its colourless aspect. Only when viewing a life in its totality, in its relation to God, do we come to know its real character.[401]

Live slowly your life: its joys and its sorrows; its toil and its rest. He must eat slowly that would digest well.[402]

Living Water

But there was more than this: it was water which forever quenched the thirst, by meeting all the inward wants of the soul; water also, which, in him who had drunk it, became a well, not merely quenching the thirst on this side time, but 'springing up into eternal life.' It was not only the material wants felt, but a new life, and that not essentially different, but the same as that of the future, and merging into it.[403]

---

399. OT, 225
400. OT, 101
401. Elisha, 285
402. Tohu, 59
403. LTJM, 285

His Quotes

The Lord's Supper

AGAIN, IF IT WERE a mere token of remembrance, why the Cup as well as the bread? . . . If we may venture an explanation, it would be that 'this' received in the Holy Eucharist, conveys to the soul as regards the Body and Blood of the Lord, the same effect as the Bread and the Wine to the body – receiving of the bread and the Cup in the Holy Communion is, really, though spiritually, to the Soul what the outward elements are to the Body: that they are both the symbol and vehicle of true, inward, spiritual feeding on the very Body and Blood of Christ.[404]

Love

WE DO NOT GIVE up the world because we are obliged to do so, but because we no longer love it, the love of the Father being now in us. Our chief motive is, not fear, but the love of Christ.[405]

IF THE LOVE OF God be really in us, our deepest earthly attachment can never come into comparison, far less into conflict with it, because it is of a totally different character . . . We do not love anything in the world, nor any creature, in the sense in which we love God; and if we were to do so, the love of the father would not be in us.[406]

THE QUESTION NOW IS not 'Who is my neighbor?' but 'Whose neighbor am I?' The Gospel answers the question of duty by pointing us to love.[407]

LOVE BENDS TO OUR need: this is the objective manifestation of the Gospel. Need looks up to love, and by its cry elicits the boon which it seeks.[408]

---

404. LTJM, 827
405. Elijah, 76
406. Elisha, 134
407. LTJM, 640
408. LTJM, 640

AND THIS – SHAME on us as we write it! – was to be the mark to all men of their discipleship.[409]

LOVE IS NOT SELF-CONSCIOUS. Why should our love to God be always self-inspective?[410]

LOVE IS THE HIGHEST of all, because it contains nothing of the negative – not the mental limitation of faith (not seeing), nor the moral limitation of hope (as implying an element of doubt), but is altogether positive and unlimited.[411]

Lying

UNTRUTH CONSISTS NOT ONLY in saying what in the wording of it is contrary to fact; but what, though perhaps literally true, leaves on the mind of another a different impression from that which we know to be the correct one.[412]

THE MORAL WRONG OF lying consists in this: that it involves the loss of personal responsibility. A person who tells 'a story' loses the sense of being personally responsible.[413]

Marriage

AT THE SAME TIME it must be born in mind, that marriage conveyed to the Jews much higher thoughts than merely those of festivity and merriment. The pious fasted before it, confessing their sins. It was regarded almost as a sacrament. Entrance into the married state was thought to carry the forgiveness of sins. It almost seems as if the relationship of Husband and Bride between Jehovah and His people, so frequently insisted upon, not

---

409. LTJM, 825
410. Tohu, 8
411. Tohu, 68
412. Elisha, 181
413. Tohu, 61

Mary

THE THREE SUBSIDIARY REASONS may once more be indicated here in explanation of the Virgin-Mother's seeming ignorance of her Son's true character: the necessary gradualness of such a revelation; the necessary development of His own consciousness; and the fact, that Jesus could not have been subject to His parents, nor had true and proper human training, if they had clearly known that he was the essential Son of God.[415]

Masada

EVENING WITH ITS CALM and silence settled on the scene around. The stars twinkled just as they had done in happier days over the burning walls of Masada. Beneath rolled heavily the Dead Sea – the monument of former wrath and woe; in the distance, so far as the eye could reach, the desolate landscape bore the marks of the oppressor. Before them was the camp of the Roman, who watched with eager anxiety for his prey and the morrow. All was silent in Masada.[416]

Matzah (unleavened bread)

THIS IS CALLED IN scripture 'the bread of affliction' (Deut 16:3), as is commonly supposed, because its insipid taste symbolised the hardship and affliction of Egypt. But this explanation must be erroneous. It would convert one of the most joyous festivals into an annual season of mourning. The idea intended to be conveyed by the Scriptural term is quite different. For, just as we should ever remember the death of our Saviour in con-

---

414. LTJM, 244
415. LTJM, 173
416. Nation, 42

nection with His resurrection, so were Israel always to remember their bondage in connection with their deliverance.[417]

Melchizadek

MELCHIZADEK APPEARS LIKE A meteor in the sky – suddenly, unexpectedly, mysteriously – and then as suddenly disappears.[418]

WHAT LAY IN GERM in Melchizadek was to be gradually unfolded – the priesthood in Aaron, the royalty in David – till both were most gloriously united in Christ.[419]

Mercy

THERE IS NOT A truth more clearly or repeatedly stated in Scripture, nor more fully borne out by the records of the past, than that of God's absolute willingness to receive *all* that come unto Him.[420]

YET THE LORD IS merciful, and full of compassion. How often in our tangled path does He guide our faltering steps![421]

GOD'S GREAT JUDGMENTS, WHEN viewed from another point, are always seen to be attended with wider manifestations of mercy. It is never judgment only, but judgment and mercy – and every movement is a movement forward, even though in making it there should be a crushing down and a breaking down.[422]

---

417. Temple, 197
418. OT, 60
419. OT, 61
420. Elisha, 248
421. True, 270
422. OT, 872

His Quotes

I can say a great many things in favour of the Lord Jesus Christ – of his Power, Grace, and Love. But the greatest I can say of them is: that he has received *me*. Thus the faith of the poorest sinner brings the greatest glory to Christ.[423]

Messianic Hope

In truth it scarcely seems exaggeration to say, that throughout the history of Israel we can trace the times of bitterest sorrows by their brightest messianic expectations, as if that golden harvest waved richest where the ploughshares had drawn the furrows deepest, and the precious seed been watered by blood and tears.[424]

If the Messianic hope had sprung up during or immediately after the exile, we should scarcely have expected it to cluster round the house of David, nor to centre in the 'Son of David.'[425]

We all start not without preconceived opinions, as some would call them – or guiding principles, as I would designate them. The Jew starts with his preconceived opinions as to what must or must not be in accordance with his general views of the teaching of the Old Testament. The Christian starts with the historical facts concerning Christ and Christianity in his mind. To the one *this*, to the other *that* is the guiding principle in the application of what both have agreed to be the meaning of the words and contents of a prophecy. And it cannot well be otherwise. The honest inquirer can only seek which of the two directions is the right one.[426]

The difference between the Messianic hope of the Old Testament and of the later time was that between the utterances of inspired men who spoke the message of God, and uninspired men who spoke of it with the

---

423. Tohu, 20
424. Prophecy, 9
425. Prophecy, 17
426. Prophecy, 108

feelings of personal injury burning in their hearts, and the thoughts of the times dominating and moulding the expression of their views.[427]

Messianic Prophecies

IT HAS BEEN WELL remarked, that the difficulties of modern interpreters of the Messianic prophecies arise chiefly from their not perceiving the unity of the Old Testament in its progressive unfolding of the plan of salvation. Moses must not be read independently of the Psalms, not yet the Psalms independently of the Prophets.[428]

IN THE NEW TESTAMENT prophecies are not made to point to facts, but facts to point back to prophecies. The New Testament presents the fulfillment of all prophecy rather than prophecies, and individual predictions serve as fingerposts to great out-standing facts, which mark where the roads meet and part.[429]

SO FAR AS WE can gather from the Gospel narratives, no objection was ever taken to the fulfillment of individual prophecies in Jesus. But the general conception which the Rabbis had formed of the Messiah, differed totally from what was presented by the Prophet of Nazareth.[430]

THE MESSIAH AND HIS history are not presented in the Old Testament as something separate from, or superadded to, Israel. The history, the institutions, and the predictions of Israel run up into Him. He is the typical Israelite, nay, typical Israel itself – alike the crown, the completion, and the representative of Israel.[431]

THEIR NUMBER AMOUNTS TO upwards of 456 (75 from the Pentateuch, 243 from the Prophets, and 138 from the hagiographa), and their Messianic

427. Prophecy, 318
428. Temple, 90
429. LTJM, xiii
430. LTJM, 113
431. LTJM, 114

application is supported by more than 558 references to the most ancient Rabbinic writings.[432]

ALL THE OLD TESTAMENT institutions, prophecies, and promises, so far as they referred to access into God's fold, meant Christ.[433]

IT IS IN THIS manner that prophecy in its application to Christ should be studied: first, the living Person, then His portraiture; first, the fulfillment, then the prophetic reference; first, the historical, then the exegetical argument. These remarks are not intended to deprecate the application of individual prophecies to Christ; only to correct a one-sided and mechanical literalism that exhausts itself in fruitless verbal controversies in which it is not unfrequently worsted, and to give to our views the right and, as we believe, the spiritual direction.[434]

Ministry (serving God)

THERE IS OFTEN MORE accomplished by stillness in God than by what seems to the world the most active and successful work.[435]

THERE ARE, ALAS, FAR too few who will not only do, but dare, for Christ.[436]

THERE ARE TIMES WHEN even prayer seems unbelief, and only to go forward in calm assurance is duty.[437]

AS IN EVERY OTHER case, so in this, God would give the person called to most difficult work every opportunity of knowing His will, and every encouragement to do it.[438]

432. LTJM, 115
433. LTJM, 606
434. Prophecy, 113
435. Golden, 74
436. Golden, 172
437. OT, 188
438. OT, 440

If the Lord has work for us, He will call us to it. But we must cultivate a spirit of attentive, prayerful readiness.[439]

With the call of Christ comes always the decisive question: Are we really willing to follow after Him, not as of necessity, nor from a painful sense of duty, but of a ready mind and a joyous heart, choosing Christ as our portion, and deeming His reproach greater riches than the treasures of Egypt?

Why should we serve the Lord with that which has cost us neither labour, study, nor preparation? *Beaten* oil was required for the temple-lamp; why then should its quality be now deemed a matter of small importance?[440]

Ministers change, but the work remains unchanged. None of us is really needed.[441]

It is this daily and hourly service which is real service. There are more martyrs in cottages, humble homes, and in every day life – more witnesses for the Christ by suffering – than those whose names are recorded on the pages of history.[442]

We cannot pay a minister; the object is to give him the means of support, that he may be able to give himself to the work of the Lord. God alone pays ministers, whether faithful or unfaithful.[443]

Sometimes God enlarges our opportunities. Such increase should be received, not in a spirit of self-congratulations, but with gratitude, with meekness, and with fear.[444]

---

439. Elisha, 7
440. Elisha, 18
441. Elisha, 33
442. Elisha, 83
443. Elisha, 180
444. Elisha, 187

His Quotes

It is wonderful how much can be accomplished by hearty, cheerful laborers, where each is ready to undertake his own share, and all are content with humble appearances, provided the great object be attained.[445]

But God often chooses what to us would seem the most unlikely instruments; instruments as unconscious of their work as the tools in the workman's hands, that so the work may be seen to be of Him, and the glory all His.[446]

Every Christian has not only work to do, but a special work is assigned to him by the appointment of God, and another cannot do it for him.[447]

Miracles

The age of miracles is not passed so long as the God of miracles liveth.[448]

It needs not special miracles where there is a constant miracle.[449]

But, in general, not to speak of the "need be" of teaching by miracles in the times of old, the miraculous is the necessary light upon what is called the Covenant-History, that is, on the record of God's dealings with His people of old . . . Thus the miraculous is not outside of, forms not an addition to, but is an essential and integral part of the history of the Old Testament and of the people of God.[450]

It were, indeed, an absurd demand to *prove* a miracle, since to do so were to show that it was not a Miracle. But we may be rationally asked these three things: first, to show, that no other explanation is rationally

---

445. Elisha, 187
446. Elisha, 245
447. Elisha, 254
448. Golden, 128
449. Golden, 175
450. Elisha, x

possible than that which proceeds on the grounds of it being a miracle; secondly, to show, that such a view of it is consistent with itself and with all the details of the narrative; and thirdly that it is harmonious with what precedes and what follows the narrative.[451]

ACCORDING TO THE GOSPELS, a man might either seek benefit from Christ, or else receive Christ through such benefit.[452]

THE ANCIENT WORLD AS much expected an argument from the miraculous, as we from the purely rational and logically evidential. But advancing civilisation has changed all this, and banished the miraculous from the sphere of ordinary thinking. Accordingly, a miracle would now, logically speaking, be a real interference, not only with the course of nature, but with our laws and habits of thinking. It can therefore no longer be God's mode of teaching to us.[453]

Monarchy

TAKING A VIAL OF oil, [Samuel] "anointed" Saul, thus placing the institution of royalty on the same footing as that of the sanctuary and the priesthood as appointed and consecrated by God and for God, and intended to be the medium for receiving and transmitting to His people.[454]

Money

BUT TO ADMONISH THE rich not to trust in uncertain riches, not to give of their means as if they were their own, but to offer as unto the Lord, meekly and in deepest humility, praying that he may be pleased to accept it; to do this, not seeking any personal advantage, is not interference, but Christian duty, and mostly a hard and trying duty to perform.[455]

451. LTJM, 689
452. LTJM, 703
453. Tohu, 50
454. OT, 436
455. Elisha, 108

His Quotes

For, strange as it may sound these days, the reception of contributions is not the highest aim to be sought by Christians. There is something much higher than this – the good of souls and the glory of God.[456]

There is not perhaps a more heartless, odious, nor, for that matter of it, a more untrue phrase than that so persistently flaunted in our faces, that notwithstanding its silliness, we almost come to receive it: business *is* business![457]

Morality

In the case of heathenism every advance in civilization has marked a progressive lowering of public morality, the earlier stages of national life always showing a far higher tone than the later. On the contrary, the religion of the Bible (under the old as under the new dispensation) has increasingly raised, if not uniformly the public morals, yet always the tone and standard of public morality; it has continued to exhibit a standard never yet attained, and it has proved its power to control public and social life, to influence and to mould it.[458]

Moses

Moses was the first to bear a Divine commission to others. He was also the first one to work miracles. All miracles pointed forward to the greatest of all miracles, "the mystery of the godliness, into which angels desire to look:" the union of the divine with the human, in its fullest appearance in the Person of the God-man. Thus in these two aspects of his office, as well as in his mission to redeem Israel from bondage and to sanctify them unto the Lord, Moses was an eminent type of Christ.[459]

---

456. Elisha, 172
457. True, 212
458. Sketches, 115
459. OT, 168

Music

THE MUSIC OF THE Temple owed its origin to David, who was not only a poet and a musical composer, but who also invented musical instruments (Amos 6:5, 1 Chron. 23:5), especially the ten stringed *Nevel* or lute (Ps 33:2, 144:9).[460]

The Nativity

IF WE THINK OF Jesus as the Messiah from heaven, the surroundings of outward poverty, so far from detracting, seem most congruous to His Divine character. Earthly splendor would have seemed like tawdry tinsel, and the utmost simplicity like that clothing of the lilies, which far surpassed all the glory of Solomon's court.[461]

WOULD JEWISH LEGEND HAVE ever presented its Messiah as born in a stable, to which chance circumstances had consigned His Mother? The whole current of Jewish opinion would run in the contrary direction. The opponents of the authenticity of this narrative are bound to face this.[462]

THAT ON SUCH SLENDER thread, as the feeble throb of an Infant-life, the salvation of the world should hang – and no special care watch over its safety, no better shelter be provided it than a 'stable,' no other cradle than a manger! And still it is ever so. On what slender thread has the continued life of the Church often seemed to hang; on what feeble throbbing that of every child of God – with no visible outward means to ward off danger, no home of comfort, no rest of ease.[463]

---

460. Temple, 150
461. LTJM, 129
462. LTJM 131
463. LTJM, 133

His Quotes

Nature

WHEN WE LOOK UP to those starry worlds above, which pursue their course in a silence of which the solemnity is almost overpowering, and whose glittering light comes through centuries and over distances which the mind may calculate, but cannot realise; when we consider what forces are perpetually at work, and what a small place and part in this vast universe our earth occupies, our hearts are well-nigh overwhelmed.[464]

SINCE THE FALL, WE read nature, at best, only by night-light.[465]

THERE ARE SILENT SERMONS delivered all day and all night in every place . . . Far away from home and its privileges, has the missionary been long preceded by silent preachers, who speak to him as they do to those who understand not their teaching.[466]

THERE IS SO MUCH of promise in all nature, of beauty and wealth yet undeveloped, but ready to break from a bondage which can no longer hold it, that we insensibly share as it were the universal hope that is about to burst into reality all around , in hedge and tree, in field and meadow.[467]

Nazareth

MEN OF ALL NATIONS, busy with another life than that of Israel, would appear in the streets of Nazareth; and through them thoughts, associations, and hopes connected with the great outside world be stirred. But, on the other hand, Nazareth was also one of the great centers of Jewish Temple-life. It has already been indicated that the priesthood was divided into twenty-four 'courses,' which, in turn, ministered in the Temple . . . Now Nazareth was one of these priest-centers, and although it may well have been, that comparatively few in distant Galilee conformed to the

---

464. Elijah, 81
465. Golden, 55
466. Golden, 152
467. True, 249

priestly regulations – some must have assembled there in preparation for the sacred functions, or appeared in its Synagogue.[468]

IF, THEREFORE, FOR REASONS easily comprehended, the mystery of His incarnation was not to be divulged, it was needful that the Incarnate of Nazareth should be born in Bethlehem, and the infant of Bethlehem be brought up in Nazareth.[469]

Nicodemus

A NICODEMUS IS SPOKEN of in the Talmud as one of the richest and most distinguished citizens of Jerusalem . . . But there can scarcely be a doubt that this somewhat legendary *Naqdimon* was *not* the Nicodemus of the Gospel.[470]

THROUGHOUT, JESUS NEVER DESCENDED to the standpoint of Nicodemus, but rather sought to lift him to His own.[471]

WHAT NICODEMUS HAD SEEN of Jesus had not only shaken the confidence which his former views on these subjects had endangered him, but opened dim possibilities, the very suggestion of which filled him with uneasiness as to the past, and vague hopes as to the future. And so it ever is with us also, when, like Nicodemus, we first arrive at the conviction that Jesus is the Teacher come from God.[472]

Noah

THE STATEMENT THAT NOAH found grace is like the forth-bursting of the sun in a sky lowering for the storm.[473]

    468. LTJM, 104
    469. LTJM, 438
    470. LTJM, 263
    471. LTJM, 265
    472. LTJM, 266
    473. OT, 28

His Quotes

THUS THE GREAT FAITH of Noah appeared not only in building an ark in the midst of a scoffing and unbelieving generation, and that against all human probability of its ever been needed, and one hundred and twenty years before it was actually required, but in providing room for "his sons" and his "sons' wives," while as yet he himself was childless![474]

THE DIFFERENCE BETWEEN NOAH and Elijah was only that of time and circumstances: the one was before, the other after the giving of the law; the one was sent into an apostate world, the other to an apostatizing covenant-people.[475]

Old Testament

WE TURN AGAIN TO the Old Testament, and in regard to it claim to have established these positions: that the Old Testament itself pointed to spiritual realities of which the external and the then present were confessedly and consciously the symbols. And, secondly, that in this it pointed for the fulfillment of all the 'latter' or Messianic days.[476]

Opposition

WHEN WE PLACE OURSELVES on God's side, the malice of our enemies is alike folly and sin.[477]

THESE ARE DAYS IN which believers are more especially exposed to the sneers of the world and mockery is more difficult to bear than even persecution.[478]

---

474. OT, 28
475. OT, 667
476. Propecy, 181
477. Golden, 19
478. Golden, 116

We are far too fearful of the haters of the Lord. Their power equals not their purpose. He holds them in rein Who at any moment can arrest them. Most of our perils exist in apprehension only.[479]

For, opposition ever brings into clearer light positive truth, just as judgment comes never alone, but always conjoined with display of Higher mercy.[480]

Original Sin

It was neither at the feet of Gamaliel, nor yet from Jewish Hellenism, that Saul of Tarsus learned the doctrine of original sin. The statement that in Adam all spiritually died, so in Messiah all should be made alive, finds absolutely no parallel in Jewish writings.[481]

Of course, it is not meant that [the Rabbis] denied the consequences of sin, either as concerned Adam himself, or his descendants; but the final result is far from that seriousness which attaches to the Fall in the New Testament, where it is presented as the basis of the need of a Redeemer, Who, as the Second Adam, restored what the first had lost.[482]

Passover

Any attempt at describing either Israel's attitude or the scenes witnessed when the Lord, passing through the land "about midnight," smote each firstborn from the only son of Pharaoh to the child of the maidservant and the captive, and even the firstborn of beasts, would only weaken the impression of the majestic silence of Scripture.[483]

---

479. Golden, 182
480. LTJM, 359
481. LTJM, 36
482. LTJM, 116
483. OT, 185

His Quotes

Just as the Priesthood of Christ was real, yet not after the order of Aaron, so was the Sacrifice of Christ real, yet not after the order of Levitical sacrifices but after that of the Passover.[484]

Jewish tradition has this curious conceit: that the most important events in Israel's history were connected with the paschal season.[485]

As the present Passover liturgy contains comparatively few relics from New Testament times, so also the present arrangement of the paschal table evidently dates from a time when sacrifices had ceased. On the other hand, however, by far the greater number of the usages observed in our own days are precisely the same as eighteen hundred years ago.[486]

The Paschal is by far the happiest of Israel's festivals. In general, there is nothing morose nor austere about the observances which Jehovah has enjoined upon His people. Each feast is an occasion of joy and thanksgiving. At every festival, not isolated worshippers, but all the families of Israel, are, as such, to take part in the service and gladness. Isolation and individualism are alike contrary to the spirit of our religion. God deals with us as with families. We do not come as separate individuals, offering an isolated service; age, rank, and sex do not make any difference. As families we share in the blessing and in the joy.[487]

One by one the stars sprung up on the evening sky, showing as it were, by contrast, its rich deep blue. Each company now gathered around its own table. Costly carpets covered the floors; the scent of richest perfume pervaded the apartments. The women were elegantly dressed; children flitted to and fro in joyous excitement. Servants and maids came in to the table as Israelites, and holding the same place on the great festival of our national deliverance as their masters.[488]

---

484. LTJM, 814
485. Temple, 180
486. Temple, 182
487. Scattered, 1870, Grey to Dawn, p. 6
488. Scattered, 1870, Grey to Dawn, p. 6

Patience

If only men continued to wait upon the Lord, how many buds, killed by the storm, would have opened into blossom and ripened into precious fruit![489]

Patriarchs

Thus "Abraham was the man of joyous, working faith; Isaac of patient, bearing faith; and Jacob of contending and prevailing faith."[490]

Let it be borne in mind, that God had both made and established His covenant with Abraham. The history of Isaac and Jacob, on the other hand, rather represents *the hindrances of the covenant*. These are just the same as we daily meet in our own walk of faith. They arise from opposite causes, according as in our weakness we either lag behind, or in our haste go before God.[491]

Paul

Yet Saul of Tarsus was a Jew, not merely trained at the feet of the great Gamaliel, "that sun in Israel," but deeply imbued with the Jewish spirit and lore; insomuch that long afterwards, when he is writing of the deepest mysteries of Christianity, we catch again and again expressions that remind us of some that occur in the earliest record of that secret Jewish doctrine, which was only communicated to the most select of the select sages.[492]

---

489. Elisha, 314
490. OT, 51
491. OT, 79
492. Sketches, 172

His Quotes

THE MODERN SYNAGOGUE HATES St. Paul as much as the ancient Synagogue hated Jesus Christ. This affords, I think, proof that he was a true Apostle.[493]

IN ST. PAUL'S WRITINGS, dogmatics and practical religion absolutely coincide. Each is also the other. A lesson, this, to us.[494]

HIS LETTERS, READ FAIRLY, carry to the mind the conviction that in heart, affection, and sympathy, he was with his Jewish brethren – all but in their sad and fatal unbelief. His mode of reasoning and expression, his illustrations, often the very terms which he uses are all Jewish; and for ourselves we wish no better than to follow the great Apostle of the Gentiles in his Jewish, as well as in his Christian sympathies.[495]

Peace

NO MAN EVER FOUND peace by seeking *it* primarily; every man may find it by seeking Christ.[496]

Pentecost

THE DAY OF PENTECOST was God's morning greeting to the Church.[497]

Pentateuch

BUT WHAT WE HAVE to insist upon is the general trustfulness and reliableness of the Book, alike as regards its history and legislation: that it is, what

---

493. Tohu, 105
494. Tohu, 128
495. Watchman, March 1877, p. 1
496. Golden, 208
497. Tohu, 127

it professes, an authentic record of the history of Israel, and a trustworthy account of what was really the Mosaic legislation.[498]

THE MORE WE THINK of the spirit and of the details of the Mosaic legislation, the stronger grows our conviction, that such laws and institutions could have been only introduced before the people actually settled in the land.[499]

Peter

WE NEED NOT INQUIRE which of the slightly varying reports in the Gospels represents the actual words of the woman or the actual answer of Peter. Perhaps neither; perhaps all – certainly, she said all this, and, certainly, he answered all that, though neither of them would confine their words to the short sentences reported by each of the Evangelists.[500]

Pharisees

COURTED OR FEARED, SHUNNED or flattered, reverently looked up to or laughed at, he was equally a power everywhere, both ecclesiastically and politically, as belonging to the most closely-connected religious fraternity, which in the pursuit of its objects spared neither time nor trouble, feared no danger, and shrunk from no consequences.[501]

INDEED, THE SAYINGS OF some of the Rabbis in regard to Pharisaism and the professional Pharisee are more withering than any in the New Testament.[502]

---

498. Prophecy, 231
499. Sketches, 186
500. LTJM, 855
501. Sketches, 195
502. LTJM, 217

His Quotes

Philo

It is strange how little we know of the personal history of the greatest of uninspired Jewish writers of old, though he occupied so prominent a position in his time. Philo was born in Alexandria, about the year 20 before Christ. He was a descendant of Aaron, and belonged to one of the wealthiest and most influential families among the Jewish merchant-princes of Egypt.[503]

To begin with, Philo united in rare measure Greek learning with Jewish enthusiasm. In his writings he frequently uses classical modes of expression; he names not fewer than sixty-four Greek writers; and he either alludes to, or quotes frequently from, such sources as Homer, Hesiod, Pindar, Solon, the great Greek tragedians, Plato, and others. But to him these men were scarcely 'heathen.' He had sat at their feet, and learned to weave a system from Pythagoras, Plato, Aristotle, and the Stoics. The gatherings of the philosophers were 'holy,' and Plato was 'the great.' But holier than all was the gathering of true Israel; and incomparably greater than any, Moses.[504]

The *doctrinal* views of Philo may briefly be characterized as a mixture of Platonism and Jewish mysticism.[505]

The last word of Philo's philosophy, like that of the Kabbala is – Pantheism.[506]

Pliny

Moreover, it must be kept in view that according to Pliny, it was distinctive of these same Christians rather to suffer martyrdom than to offer even the supposed inferior homage to the Roman Emperor, although

---

503. LTJM, 28
504. LTJM, 28
505. Nation, 448
506. Nation, 449

they fully owned his supreme civil authority. Hence the Christian worship of Jesus must have been consciously and literally offered to Christ as a Divine Person.[507]

Pluralism

WE HAVE OUR OWN principles, so it is argued, and others have their views. There need be no collision. On these points we may agree to differ, a saying which may be ranked among those specious platitudes, by which the great Enemy has deceived and injured so many. What! Agree to differ! On what subject? Whether Jehovah or Baal is God? Yes, we shall differ, but never *agree* to differ on this point, till our faithfulness and strength have disappeared under the insidious influence of slow but certain spiritual poison.[508]

Politics

POLITICS AND RELIGION – what have they in common? This fundamental principle: "The Lord Reigneth."[509]

SIMILARLY, IT BECOMES US, in these days of party-strife and contention, to be on guard against identifying religion with one or another political movement or party. As Christian men, we are bound to take a Christian view of all questions which concern the public welfare.[510]

CHRIST'S KINGDOM IS NOT of this world; a true theocracy is not inconsistent with submission to the secular power in things that are truly its own; politics and religion neither include, nor yet exclude, each other; they are, side by side, in different domains. The State is Divinely sanctioned, and

---

507. Prophecy, 97
508. Elisha, 62
509. Elisha, 196
510. Elisha, 295

religion is Divinely sanctioned – and both are equally the ordinance of God.[511]

I LIKE A REPUBLIC, but I detest a democracy.[512]

Pontius Pilate

BUT THESE WORDS STRUCK only a hollow void, as they fell on Pilate. It was not merely cynicism, but utter despair of all that is higher – a moral suicide – which appears in his question: 'What is truth?' he had understood Christ, but it was not in him to respond to His appeal. He, Whose heart and life had so little kinship to 'the truth,' could not sympathise with, though he dimly perceived, the grand aim of Jesus' life and Work. But even the question of Pilate seems an admission, an implied homage to Christ. Assuredly, he would not have so opened his inner being to one of the priestly accusers of Jesus.[513]

Poverty

WHY ARE WE SO prone always to lay the existence of such a class to the charge of *society* in general and of our institutions? Would the class disappear, whatever changes were introduced into our social arrangements? and is its presence, at least in most instances, not due to *moral* causes rather than to outward circumstances? And if so, does not the chief blame really lie, not with society, nor with our institutions, so much as with Christians, who, possessing in the gospel of Jesus the only radical cure for moral evil, are unfaithful to their trust, and neglect their opportunities?[514]

---

511. LTJM, 740
512. Tohu, 7
513. LTJM, 868
514. True, 154

The Wisdom of Alfred Edersheim

Prayer

All men pray at some time; God's people only pray at *all* times.[515]

For the assurance that we are always heard, makes us not only the more earnest in calling, but the more humble in beseeching, knowing why and how we are accepted.[516]

For nothing more clearly marks our absolute confidence than to bring our questions to Him, instead of attempting to answer or suppress them.[517]

There are people who cry unto the Lord and are not heard. But why? Because when they called upon the Lord, they praised Him not, but resisted Him.[518]

It sometimes seems to us, in times of trouble, as if we had scarcely ever known before the value of prayer. So fresh, so great and so comforting is the privilege felt, that we wonder how we so rarely went to, and so little remained at the throne of grace.[519]

Prayer begins at nothing and ends with everything. The very idea of prayer implies my utter poverty and His infinite riches.[520]

Answered prayer gives confidence for the future, comfort for the past, and deliverance from present distress. Want of *joyous* assurance in prayer makes prayer itself a dull, formal, irksome duty. There can not be

---

515. Golden, 16
516. Golden, 19
517. Golden, 65
518. Golden, 136
519. Golden, 167
520. Golden, 168

uncertainty on this subject. God for Christ's sake *always* hears prayer – every prayer, even the faintest cry. Let us ever remember that this is our peculiar privilege under the dispensation of grace.[521]

As MIRACLE IS NOT magic, so prayer is not necessitarianism; and on looking back upon our lives we have to thank God as often for prayers unanswered as for prayers answered.[522]

To OPEN OUR WHOLE heart to God; to tell Him all we need, not only in things spiritual but in things temporal; to spread before the Lord all that concerns us and others, is indeed not only our highest privilege, but our greatest happiness.[523]

PRAYER, UNLIMITED IN ITS possibilities, stands midway between heaven and earth; with one hand it reaches up to heaven, with the other down to earth; in it, faith prepares to receive, what charity is ready to dispense.[524]

THE BELIEVER MAY, INDEED, ask for anything, because he may always and absolutely go to God; but the certainty of special answers to prayer is proportionate to the degree of union and communion with Christ.[525]

To BECOME, AND NOT always *to get* – such should be our motto in prayer. May not the opposite explain much of the poverty in prayer?[526]

---

521. Golden, 287
522. OT, 939
523. Elisha, 86
524. LTJM, 733
525. LTJM, 834
526. Tohu, 18

Preaching

NOT EVERYONE IS CALLED to be a preacher by word. But we all may, and ought to be, preachers by deed. A life that teaches how to live, and how to die, yet so as not to die, is a useful, noble life.[527]

WHY ARE PREACHERS IN the habit of asking a series of questions in the pulpit when they immediately add: These are questions which we cannot answer? What can be the use of publicly asking a question which on your own showing you cannot answer?[528]

Prejudice

THE IMPROBABILITY OF A story rarely prevents its reception by the populace, especially if their prejudices or their passions are in any way in favor of it.[529]

The Prophets

THE PRESENCE OF THE prophet in Israel meant the final call of God to Israel, and the possibility of national repentance and forgiveness.[530]

THE PROPHET, SO TO speak, translates the vernacular of the present into Divine language of the future, and he interprets the Divine sayings concerning the future by the well-known language of the present.[531]

FOR, THIS IS CHARACTERISTIC of the Prophet: not that he merely foretold the future, nor yet that he admonished as from God in regard to the present, nor even that he combined these two; but that he foretold the future

---

527. Elisha, 323
528. Tohu, 83
529. Nation, 65
530. OT, 795
531. OT, 832

on its bearing on the present, and spake of the present as viewing it in the light of the future, and that he did both as commissioned of God, inspired by God, and working for God.[532]

For, this was the first, in one sense the only, qualification for the prophetic office – to obey the Lord literally, to do and to say not less and not more than the Lord directed.[533]

There is a moral aspect in prophecy to all generations. Under one aspect of it, it prepares for the future, and this is the predictive element of it. Under its other aspect it teaches lessons of the present to each generation; and this is its moral aspect.[534]

Prophecy, in general – perhaps I should have said Prophetism – may, in the Biblical sense of the term, be defined as the reflection upon earth of the Divine ideal in its relation to the course of human affairs.[535]

We no longer regard the prophet as merely the foreteller of future events, nor yet identify prophecy with prediction. This would introduce a heathen and mantic element, contrary to the whole spirit of the Old Testament, and foreign to it also in this, that it withdraws from its most important institutions the moral and spiritual, which is the primary principle of the Old Testament.[536]

If I might venture on an illustration: the reading of prophecy seems like gazing through a telescope, which is successfully drawn out in such manner as to adapt the focus to the varying visions.[537]

532. Elisha, x
533. Elisa, 16
534. Prophecy, 38
535. Prophecy, 117
536. Prophecy, 126
537. Prophecy, 129

It is not fate that presides over prophecy, nor does fatality follow it. But there is a Living and True God Who reigneth, and the moral is the rule and characteristic of all prophecy.[538]

The prophets were indeed first and foremost God's messengers; but they were also true patriots, and intensely national, and this not despite, but rather because of their office. Any national reaction, any possible prospect of national return to God, must have had their warmest sympathy and received their most hearty encouragement. In short, whenever they could, they would most readily range themselves on the side of their people and its rulers. They would co-operate whenever and in whatsoever they might; and only protest, warn, and denounce when they must.[539]

Protestant Reformation

We gladly admit that the spirit of Protestantism is opposed to all religious persecution; but that spirit has taken centuries to evolve itself in outward manifestation; nor, indeed, is the process yet complete.[540]

Sunk in vice and corruption, contemptible for their ignorance, unbearable for their pride and arrogance, the clergy of Rome had degenerated into machines for saying mass, into figures for passing in processions, into relic-mongers and indulgence-traffickers. Talent had lost itself in mere casuistry; in the garb of scholasticism, learning sat crowned with the fool's cap of sophistry and pedantry. The country was covered with swarms of begging-orders, whose worthlessness generally kept proportion with their importunity, and whose pretensions to sanctify were only outdone by their gross dissoluteness. The pulpit, if ever taunted by monk or priest, resounded with absurd legends, or gross recommendations of the wares which mother Church kept for sale. The gospel of the Lord was hid – the volume in obscure corners of musty libraries, the reality perhaps in a few wandering outcasts, or in solitary mourners. Religion's self, where still it existed, was in danger of shriveling into the morbid selfishness of

---

538. Prophecy, 153
539. OT, 856
540. Peculiar, p. 317

an ascetic mysticism, instead of expanding and stretching out its arms to embrace the nations of the earth.[541]

EVERY REFORMATORY MOVEMENT HAS two aspects: the one negative, in opposition to prevailing error; the other positive, in the explanation of some truth, or in the enforcement of some duty.[542]

IT MUST NEVER BE forgotten that a healthy reformation can only proceed gradually and step by step. If a movement is to be true and lasting, it must progress and carry along the convictions of those who share it. The goal is not reached at abound; on his weary ascent up the mountain, the traveler only gains the full prospect when he has climbed the last and crowning height.[543]

Providence

AND IT EVER IS so, that God's greatest miracle lies in this, that He brings about heavenly results by earthly means, all unheeded and unthought of, thus moving "in a mysterious way" while performing His wonders.[544]

AND IN THIS LIES the mystery of Divine Providence, that it always worketh wonders, yet without seeming to work at all – whence also it so often escapes the observation of men. Silently, and unobserved by those who live and act, it pursues its course, till in the end all things are seen "to work together" for the Glory of God, and "for good to them that love God, that are called according to his purpose."[545]

541. Reformers, 218
542. Reformers, 219
543. Reformers, 223
544. Watchman, April 1877, p. 30
545. OT, 101

When God is about to do any of His great works, He first silently prepares all for it. Not only the good seed to be scattered, but the breaking up of the soil for its reception is His.[546]

Almost had they succeeded – but that "almost," which as so often in the history of God's people, calls out earnest faith and prayer, only proves the real impotence of this world's might as against the Lord.[547]

And they who have not learned to discover providence in all things, however insignificant, have not yet understood its mystery at all, have not risen from the heathen abstraction of providence, which is only another kind of fate, to the Christian experience of a Provider.[548]

It was, surely, a wonderously linked chain of circumstances, which bound the Synagogue to the Church. Such a result could never have been foreseen, as that, what really was the consequence of Israel's dispersion, and therefore, indirectly the punishment of their sin, should become the means of fulfilling Israel's world mission. . . . For the Synagogue became the cradle of the Church. Without it, as indeed without Israel's dispersion, the Church Universal would, humanly speaking, have been impossible, and the [conversion] of the Gentiles have required a succession of millennial miracles.[549]

Speculations and wishes, however natural in the student of history, read almost like a libel on Providence; they give way before a devout consideration of the ways of God, and an enlarged view of a period. [550]

---

546. OT, 162
547. OT, 493
548. True, 214
549. LTJM, 298
550. Reformers, 265

His Quotes

Psalms

AND AS WE DEVOUTLY trace this, the great truths around us which all the Psalms seem to move come into the foreground. These are: the misery of sin, the fullness of God's salvation, and the reality of the promises as apprehended by faith.[551]

ACCORDINGLY, THE BOOK OF Psalms, which even in its fivefold division corresponds to the Pentateuch, presents the experience – the faith, hope and love – of those who, having been made members of Christ's Church, 'delight in the law of God after the inward man.'[552]

HOWEVER THE PSALMS MAY differ, in this they agree, that every one of them contains utterances of joy, for each anticipated victory and deliverance from the Lord.[553]

THE NEARER WE APPROACH the view of Calvary (Psalm 22), the more distinctively messianic do the prophetic utterances of the Psalms become. There is less of the type and more of the Antitype, till David seems lost in 'the Son of David.'[554]

HERE WE SPECIALLY MARK how frequently and emphatically the Law is referred to, not as a code of outward commandments, but in its deeper and spiritual bearing on the inward man. This especially in the Book of Psalms, which may be described as being equally of the Law and the Prophets, converting the teaching of both into spiritual life-blood.[555]

LET IT BE BORNE in mind that [the Psalms were] at the same time the liturgy, the hymnody, and in great measure the dogmatics of the Old Testament Church.[556]

551. Golden, viii
552. Golden, 2
553. Golden, 60
554. Golden, 177
555. Prophecy, 177
556. Prophecy, 189

Its grandeur of God-conception, its intense pathos of suffering, its sweet tenderness of feeling, its child-like simplicity of faith, and the absoluteness of its trustfulness, still best express our deepest religious experience.[557]

Psalm 22

This is the psalm of psalms, in which 'Christ Jesus is evidently set forth' crucified among us. There is not a passage in the Old Testament, not even Isaiah 53, in which 'the sufferings of Christ and the glory to come' are more fully delineated.[558]

So exact, indeed, is this portraiture of His sufferings when compared with the account given by the Evangelists, and of the salvation of the world as connected with His resurrected, that, as one has aptly said, we seem to read, 'not so much prophecy, as history.'[559]

And there is peculiar emphasis in the expression: 'thou art my God from my mother's belly.' We remember the history of His incarnation and the song of Mary, and it is most significant that the reference is only to His *mother*, with still higher application to His *father who is in heaven*.[560]

And how awfully faithful is the description of the crucifixion! We learn its agonies almost better from this psalm than even from the records in the Gospels.[561]

It was this combination of the Old Testament idea of sacrifice, and of the Old Testament ideal of willing suffering as the Servant of Jehovah,

---

557. Prophecy, 190
558. Golden 184
559. Golden, 186
560. Golden, 190
561. Golden, 194

now fulfilled in Christ, which found its full expression in the language of the twenty-second Psalm.[562]

Rabbi Akiva

IN THEIR EXTRAVAGANCE, THE rabbis went so far as to assert that Akiba had discovered many things of which even Moses had been ignorant. After the manner of the time, a legend related that Moses had at one time inquired of the Lord as to the meaning and purpose of the marks which he had added to the Hebrew letters in the Bible, and had in reply been informed, that after many generations Rabbi Akiba was to make them the basis of the halacha. It was added, that Moses had requested to be allowed to see his great teacher, but that he had to sit eight rows behind Rabbi Akiba (in token of his inferiority), and felt unable to comprehend the meaning of his interpretations.[563]

Rabbi Eleazer

DURING HIS STAY [IN Caesarea, late first century] he associated with some Jewish Christians, and, at one time, incurred the suspicion of having joined the Church. He was in consequence summoned before the proconsul to recant his supposed profession of the gospel. The explanations which he offered satisfied the authorities that he had never belonged to the hated sect. But Eleazer was not so easily satisfied as the Roman governor. He bitterly reproached himself for having given any ground for such suspicion, by holding intercourse with heretics.[564]

IN HYPERBOLIC LANGUAGE IT was said that "if the expanse of the heavens had been parchment, the trees of Lebanon pens, and the waters of the sea ink, all would not have sufficed to write down what Eleazer knew." [565]

562. LTJM, 891
563. Nation, 184
564. Nation, 173
565. Nation, 174

Rabbinic Teaching

And here we may mark the fundamental distinction between the teaching of Jesus and Rabbanism. He left the *halakhah* untouched, putting it, as it were, on one side, as something quite secondary, while He insisted as primary on that which to them was chiefly matter of Haggadah. . . . The one developed the Law in its outward direction and ordinances and commandments; the other in its inward application as life and liberty.[566]

Never are the voices of the Rabbis more discordant, and their utterances more contradictory or unsatisfying than in view of the great problems of humanity: sin, sickness, death, and the hereafter.[567]

Rabbinism, which was the true outcome of the post-exilian period, is, in its inmost tendency, not only anti-monarchial and anti-sacerdotal, but strange as it may sound, anti-Messianic.[568]

Beyond the four corners of its reasoning, Rabbanism acknowledges no authority whatever, on earth – be it priestly or royal – or in heaven.[569]

We may safely assume that the historic and prophetic character of the Old Testament, as preparing for, and pointing to, the Messiah, would not be seriously questioned by the Synagogue – at least by the orthodox part of it – however strenuously the fulfillment of the prophetic Scriptures in Christ might be denied.[570]

It could scarcely be imagined that at any future period Judaism, whether of the Rabbinic or rationalistic kind, would unfold into such a universal religion and Kingdom of God, as the prophets describe.[571]

566. LTJM, 74
567. Sketches, 149
568. Prophecy, 22
569. Prophecy, 23
570. Prophecy, 164
571. Prophecy, 181

His Quotes

Rabbinical formalism may, however, as a whole, be characterized as an entirely nationalistic system, i.e., as a purely logical development, designed only for the *mind*, and which presented nothing for the *heart* save bitter and sad recollections.[572]

In its general aspect Judaism was a vast system of rationalism, which, according to the bent of different minds, took the direction of traditionalism, of skepticism, or of mysticism.[573]

Reform Judaism

While messianic hopes and national prospects, as traced by the prophets, still occupy a most prominent position in the liturgies of that party, they are all but universally disavowed.[574]

A large proportion regard it rather as their misfortune than as their privilege to have descended from Abraham. Loud and earnest as their public protestations to the contrary are, many belong to Judaism from the accident of birth more than the choice of conviction . . . In sad earnest, modern Judaism, wanting all positive, distinctive elements, has, strictly speaking, no reason of being. What do reforming Jews believe in, or hope for, that, say Unitarian Christians, do not believe in or hope for? Theirs is really not Judaism, nor is it the religion of the Old Testament; it has nothing which in principle, and very little which in practice, distinguishes it from a modified Deism.[575]

572. Nation, 101
573. Nation, 408
574. Peculiar, p. 317
575. Peculiar, p. 318

Religion

Religion, to be genuine, must be of our own free and joyous, though spiritual, choice. It is not a matter of necessity, the offspring of fear of hell, but the gladsome consent of the heart to the gracious call of the Lord.[576]

Religion is in the soul; it is a transaction between God and the human heart; it is a new life imparted and nourished by the Holy Spirit. Its beginning is spiritual union to the Lord Jesus; its growth is in fellowship with Him.[577]

That religion is not worth anything which is not worth everything, and does not pervade everything.[578]

The test of real religion is, how it endureth affliction, whether it draws us closer to, or away from God; whether it softens or hardens the heart; whether it leads to repentance or to despair.[579]

So-called acts of religion may be easy; a life of religion is unattainable, except for grace.[580]

How much of what some people call their religion would be left, if fear of death and hell were removed? But a religion whose sole motive is fear, not love, cannot be either spiritual or healthy.[581]

All heathenism is based upon the idea of nationalism – every nation had its peculiar deities and rites. But true religion must necessarily not only be national but universal.[582]

---

576. Elisha, 10
577. Elisha, 37
578. Elisha, 52
579. Elisha, 69
580. Elisha, 164
581. Elisha, 221
582. Nation, 100

His Quotes

THE TWO GREAT DIFFICULTIES in religion are: the mysteries of our faith and the inconsistencies of Christians.[583]

Repentance

MAN'S REPENTANCE IMPLIES A change of mind, God's a change of circumstances and relations. *He* has not changed, but is ever the same; it is man who has changed in his position relatively to God.[584]

GOD FORBID THAT WE should deny the possibility of deathbed repentances; but we say it even more energetically: God forbid we should trust ourselves to them.[585]

Resurrection of Jesus

THAT SOME GREAT CATASTROPHE, betokening the impending destruction of the Temple, had occurred in the Sanctuary about this very time, is confirmed by not less than four mutually independent testimonies: those of Tacitus (Hist. v13), of Josephus (War 6.5.3), of the Talmud (Jer. Yoma 43c; Yoma 39b), and of earliest Christian tradition.[586]

CONSIDERING THEIR PREVIOUS STATE of mind and the absence of any motive, how are we to account for the change of mind on the part of the disciples in regard to the resurrection? There can at least be no question, that they came to believe, and with the most absolute certitude, in the Resurrection as an historical fact . . . Indeed, the world would not have been converted to a dead Jewish Christ, however his intimate disciples might have continued to love his memory.[587]

---

583. Tohu, 41
584. OT, 460
585. Elisha, 283
586. LTJM, 894
587. LTJM, 904

AND EVEN IF SLIGHT discrepancies, nay, some not strictly historical details, which might have been the outcome of earliest tradition in the Apostolic Church, could be shown in those accounts which were not of eyewitnesses, it would assuredly not invalidate the great fact itself, *which may unhesitatingly be pronounced that best established in history.*[588]

THE IMPORTANCE OF ALL this can not be adequately expressed in words. A dead Christ might have been a Teacher and Wonder-worker, and remembered and loved as such. But only a Risen and living Christ could be the Savior, the Life, and the Life-Giver – and as such preached to all men. And of this most blessed truth we have the fullest and most unquestionable evidence.[589]

A DEAD CHRIST COULD not have become the life of a dead world: the water cannot rise above its source.[590]

Return of Jesus

IF THE CHURCH SHOULD hourly be anticipant of her salvation in the return of her Lord, the world should be hourly afraid of His sudden coming.[591]

LET US DWELL WITH warm and deep affection upon that blessed truth of His coming. It is not a barren speculation, but a glorious reality, which forms alike the hope of the Church and of earth itself. Till then we must expect disorder and confusion.[592]

---

588. LTJM, 906
589. LTJM, 906
590. Tohu, 114
591. Golden, 98
592. Golden, 230

His Quotes

Revivalism

THE RELIGION OF REVIVALISM is too often like an apple roasted at a quick fire: soft and pulpy outside, hard and sour inside.[593]

Roman Rule

ABSOLUTELY FREE AS THE inhabitants of Palestine might seem to a superficial observer, the Romans had enclosed them completely within their governmental net. The net might be very wide spread, but its meshes were the closest and the strongest. Not a department of life, not a grade of society, without constant though unnoticed supervision. The Pharisee in his school, the Sadducee in his easy-going liberalism, the Essene in his wild retirement – the zealot, the nationalist, the priest, the merchant, the stranger, – all were known and watched. For taxation, in every day life, in public movements – in short, everywhere and all around, were the hated Romans, haughty, contemptuous, oppressive, unconcerned of consequences, regardless of everything but their pride and advantage, yet never forgetting that they were conquering masters, nor ever allowing others to forget it.[594]

Sabbath

THEY SADLY MISUNDERSTAND THE Lord's Day who regard it as devoted to the duties of religion as to another kind of labour. If it means anything, it means *rest* and *joy*; not bondage, but *liberty*, through, and in, and with the risen Redeemer: a being "in the Spirit" on the Lord's Day.[595]

'ALL THE DAYS OF the week,' the Rabbi says, 'has God paired, except the Sabbath, which is alone, that it may be wedded to Israel.'[596]

---

593. Tohu, 97
594. Scattered, 1869, Grey to Dawn, p. 256
595. True, 91
596. Temple, 137

ON THE OTHER HAND, the Gospels bring before us Christ more frequently on the Sabbath than on any other festive occasion. It seemed to be His special day for working the work of His Father. On the Sabbath he preached in the synagogues; he taught in the Temple; He healed the sick; he came to the joyous meal with which the Jews were wont to close the day (Luke 14:1). Yet their opposition broke out most fiercely in proportion as He exhibited the true meaning and object of the Sabbath. Never did the antagonism between the spirit and the letter more clearly appear.[597]

UNLIKE THE OTHERS OF the Ten Commandments, the Sabbath Law has in it two elements; the moral and the ceremonial: the eternal, and that which is subject to time and place; the inward and spiritual, and the outward (the one is the mode of realizing the other).[598]

THE SAVIOR HAD BROKEN their Sabbath-Law, and yet He had not broken it, for neither by remedy, nor touch, nor outward application had He healed him. He had broken the Sabbath-rest, as God breaks it, when he sends, or sustains, or restores life, or does good: all unseen and unheard, without touch or outward application, by the Word of His power, by the Presence of His life.[599]

Sacrifices

BUT SACRIFICES, IRRESPECTIVE OF a corresponding state of mind, and in rebelliousness against God, – religiousness without religion – were not only a mere *opus operatum*, but a gross caricature, essentially heathen, not Jewish.[600]

IT IS A CURIOUS fact, but sadly significant, that modern Judaism should declare neither sacrifices nor a Levitical priesthood to belong to the essence of the Old Testament; that in fact, they had been foreign elements

---

597. Temple, 150
598. LTJM, 512
599. LTJM, 516
600. OT, 461

imported into it – tolerated, indeed, by Moses, but against which the prophets earnestly protested and incessantly laboured.[601]

But thereby also the synagogue has given sentence against itself, and by disowning sacrifices has placed itself outside of the pale of the Old Testament.[602]

Every unprejudiced reader of the Bible must feel that sacrifices constitute the centre of the Old Testament.[603]

The fundamental idea of sacrifice in the Old Testament is that of substitution, which again seems to imply everything else – atonement and redemption, vicarious punishment and forgiveness.[604]

This sacrificial, vicarious, expiatory, and redemptive character of His Death, it does not explain to us, yet helps us to understand, Christ's sense of God-forsakenness in the supreme moment of the Cross; if one might so word it – the passive character of His activeness through the active character of His passiveness.[605]

Sacrifices were meaningless without brokenness of heart and spirit, and they pointed to one great sacrifice of suffering.[606]

Let us hope that the day is not far distant when all Jews will be enlightened, and be led to see that there is but One Sacrifice, and that that Sacrifice, once offered, is all-sufficient; and that neither Jew nor Gentile needs any other.[607]

601. Temple, 74
602. Temple, 75
603. Temple, 75
604. Temple, 76
605. LTJM, 891
606. Prophecy, 155
607. Modern, 103

Sadducees

THERE CAN BE NO question that the "sect" of the Sadducees originated in a reaction against the Pharisees. If the latter added to the law their own glosses, interpretations, and traditions, the Sadducee took his stand upon the bare letter of the law. He would have none of their additions and supererogations; he would not be righteous over much.[608]

Salvation

FOR THE FIRST TIME, and in the only sense, do I boast in the title – *lost* ; and eagerly do I claim to write my own name in full between these four letters, which otherwise would have been covered by those of *hell*, but now are met by those of 'seek' and 'save.'[609]

MY SALVATION IS BOUND up with His exaltation. If it is unbelief not to recognize this, it is surely misbelief not to derive comfort and joy from it.[610]

IN IT THE BIBLE sets forth at its very opening these three great ethical principles, on which rests the whole Biblical teaching concerning the Messiah and His Kingdom: that man is capable of salvation; that all evil springs from sin, with which mortal combat must be waged; and that there will be a final victory over sin through the Representative of Humanity.[611]

IF I DID NOT believe in the perseverance of the saints, I could no longer believe in the Saviour Himself. For is it not so that at our conversion we put ourselves with perfect confidence into the hands of Christ, to be saved by Him? – and salvation would scarce be worth having if, after so giving up ourselves unto Him, he could in the end leave us. [612]

608. Sketches, 222
609. Golden, 42
610. Golden, 280
611. Prophecy, 34
612. Tohu, 4

His Quotes

Samson

THE WHOLE MEANING OF Samson's history is that he was a Nazarite. His strength lay in being a Nazarite; his weakness in yielding to his carnal lusts, and thereby becoming unfaithful in his calling. In both respects he was not only a type of Israel, but, so to speak, a mirror in which Israel could see itself and its history.[613]

Samuel

PERHAPS THE MOST MAJESTIC form presented, even among the heroes of the Old Testament history, is that of Samuel, who is specially introduced to us as a man of prayer (Psa. 99:6). Levite, Nazarite, prophet, judge – each phase of his outward calling seems to have left its influence on his mind and heart.[614]

Sarah

SHE IS THE ONLY woman whose age is recorded in Scripture, the distinction being probably due to her position toward believers, as stated in 1 Peter 3:6.[615]

Satan

SATAN IS A MUCH better logician than any of us, and if we give ourselves to such calculations, it will not be difficult somehow to arrive at the conclusion, that we are at liberty to be unfaithful.[616]

---

613. OT, 381
614. OT, 425
615. OT, 73
616. Golden, 106

Earth belongs as little to Satan as the dead belong to death.[617]

The enemy of our souls ever seeks to rob us of our hope by representing our case as hopeless.[618]

The tempter always first allures, and then accuses.[619]

What Satan sought was 'My Kingdom come' – a Satanic messianic time, a Satanic Messiah; the final realization of an empire of which his present possession was only temporary, caused by the alienation of man from God. To destroy all this: to destroy the works of the Devil, to abolish his kingdom, to set man free from his domain, was the very object of Christ's Mission.[620]

Saul

Saul embodied the royal idea of the people, while David represented the Scriptural ideal of royalty in its conscious subjection to the will of the Heavenly King. Saul was, so to speak, the king after Israel's, David after God's own heart.[621]

Scribes

[The Scribe] seems ubiquitous; we meet him in Jerusalem, in Judea, and even in Galilee (Luke 5:17). Indeed, he is indispensable, not only in Babylon, which may have been the birthplace of his order, but among the 'dispersion' also. Everywhere he appears as the mouthpiece and representative of the people; he pushes to the front, the crowd respectfully giv-

---

617. Golden, 222
618. Golden, 241
619. Golden, 241
620. LTJM, 212
621. OT, 403

ing way, and eagerly hanging on his utterances, as those of a recognised authority.[622]

Scripture

FOR THE BIBLE DOES not profess to give a detailed history of the world, nor even a complete biography of those persons whom it introduces. Its object is to set before us a *history of the kingdom of God*, and it only describes such persons and events as is necessary for that purpose.[623]

THOUGH IT NEED NOT such indirect confirmations to convince us of the truth of the narratives in the Bible, it is very remarkable how all historical investigations, when really completed and rightly applied, confirm the exactness of what is recorded in the Holy Scriptures.[624]

IT NEED SCARCELY BE pointed out, how this truthful account of the sins of biblical heroes evinces the authenticity and credibility of the Scriptural narratives. Far different are the legendary accounts which seek to palliate the sins of biblical personages, or even to deny their guilt.[625]

SCRIPTURE GENEOLOGY RUNS UP into that of the Christ; Scripture miracles into His incarnation; Scripture types into his work; Scripture prophecy into His Kingdom. Therefore, when we read the Scriptures, we live not in the past.[626]

FOR HOLY SCRIPTURE, AS the communication of God to man by man, does indeed contain a distinctively human element, but that element cannot have been one of human imposture.[627]

---

622. LTJM, 65
623. OT, 15
624. OT, 34
625. OT, 538
626. Elisha, 198
627. Prophecy, 220

Septuagint

THE TRANSLATION OF THE Old Testament into Greek may be regarded as starting-point of Hellenism. It rendered possible the hope that what in its original form had been confined to a few, might become accessible to the world at large.[628]

Sermon on the Mount

WE WILL NOT DESIGNATE the 'Sermon on the Mount' as the promulgation of the New Law, since that would be a far too narrow, if not erroneous, view of it. But it certainly seems to correspond to the Divine Revelation in the 'Ten Words' from Mount Sinai.[629]

ITS GREAT SUBJECT IS neither righteousness, nor yet the New Law (if such designation be proper in regard to what in no real sense is a Law), but that which was innermost and uppermost in the Mind of Christ – the kingdom of God.[630]

TO STUDY IT MORE closely: in the three chapters, under which the Sermon on the Mount is grouped in the first Gospel (Matt. 5–7), the Kingdom of God is presented *successively, progressively,* and *extensively*.[631]

NO PART OF THE New Testament has had a larger array of Rabbinic parallels adduced then the 'Sermon on the Mount;' and this, as we might expect, because, in teaching addressed to His contemporaries, Jesus would naturally use the forms with which they were familiar. Many of these Rabbinic quotations are, however, entirely inept, the similarity lying in an expression or turn of words. Occasionally, the misleading error goes even

---

628. LTJM, 22
629. LTJM, 364
630. LTJM, 364
631. LTJM, 365

further, and that is quoted in illustration of Jesus' sayings which, either by itself or in the context, implies quite the opposite.[632]

Servant of the Lord

BUT WHAT THE NATION was, as a whole, that Israel's theocratic king was *pre-eminently*: the servant of the Lord (1 Kings 8:25, 28 29, 52, 59).[633]

BRIEFLY, THE UNDERLYING IDEA of the Old Testament, in its subjective aspect, is that of "the Servant of the Lord." The history of the Old Testament in its progress to the new is that of the widening of the idea of the servant of the Lord into that of the kingdom of God.[634]

IN THE OLD TESTAMENT, to adopt a beautiful figure, the idea of the Servant of the Lord is set before us like a pyramid: at its base it is all Israel, at the central section Israel after the Spirit (the circumcised in heart), represented by David the man after God's own heart; while at its apex it is the 'Elect' Servant, the Messiah.[635]

MOREOVER, THE MESSIAH, AS Representative Israelite, combined in Himself as '*the* Servant of the Lord' the threefold office of Prophet, Priest, and King, and joined together the two ideas of 'Son' and 'Servant' (Phil 2:6-11). And the final combination and full exhibition of these two ideas was the fulfillment of the typical mission of Israel, and the establishment of the Kingdom of God among men.[636]

---

632. LTJM, 367
633. OT, 603
634. OT, 832
635. LTJM, 38
636. LTJM, 114

Shakespeare

Had Shakespeare drawn his character of Shylock from any of the inhabitants from the Ghetto, he would have rightly represented a class, instead of having libeled a nation.[637]

Shepherd

A sweeter or more precious designation of Christ than that of 'Shepherd' Scripture itself does not contain. It expresses His work *for* us, by which He purchased us to be His flock, and His work *in* us and *with* us, by which He taketh us in charge and careth for us.[638]

Sin

Sin is ever its own curse, and rebellion its own punishment.[639]

The approach of sin is as slow as it is deceptive.[640]

Whenever and wherever a sin is very widely indulged in, even believers seem to lose their intense sensibility concerning it. The atmosphere which they breathe has become so poisoned as to have influenced their system.[641]

In our carnality we are ever prone to judge things by their visible consequences, and thus our fundamental sin is least noticed or made account of. We are concerned in proportion as we *see* the affects of our sin – and this is another proof of our practical atheism.[642]

---

637. Modern, 112
638. Golden, 206
639. Golden, 9
640. Golden, 52
641. Golden, 67
642. Golden, 95

His Quotes

I shall best learn the corruption of human nature by studying it in itself. 'For out of the heart proceed evil thoughts, murders, adulteries, fornication, theft, false witnesses, blasphemies,' – in short, the whole catalogue of breaches of both tables of the law.[643]

But should not all this teach us, that, however necessary a deep and true sense of guilt and sin may be, yet if sin pardoned continueth sin brooded over, it becomes a source, not of sanctification, but of moral weakness and hindrance?[644]

Any practice, however indifferent in itself, becomes absolutely sinful, when, ceasing to be indifferent, it is made the object of superstition to our neighbor.[645]

Yet each of us has a lack – something quite deep down in our hearts, which we may never yet have known, and which we must know and give up, if we would follow Christ. And without forsaking, there can be no following. This is the law of the Kingdom – and it is such, because we are sinners, because sin is not only the loss of the good, but the possession of something in its place.[646]

When a sense of sin has been awakened in us, we shall mourn, not for what Christ has suffered, but for what He suffered for us.[647]

It is not the sinner, but the sinning, who should tremble.[648]

---

643. Golden, 100
644. OT, 557
645. Elisha, 176
646. LTJM, 710
647. LTJM, 879
648. Tohu, 22

Skeptics

Thus while men continually raise fresh objections against Holy Scripture, those formerly so confidently relied upon have been removed by further researches, made quite independently of the Bible, just as an enlarged knowledge will sweep those urged in our days.[649]

Every age has produced its new objectors and its fresh objections; and every host has been alike confident of success. They think that those who before them had gone to the attack, had not striven to beset every gate and postern. But they deceive themselves and are deceived. Every point of attack has been attempted and failed. Now the authority of the Old Testament, then that of the New, has been called in question . . . But by what formula do these men, who boast of destroying our hope, who will turn to current of the river of life, and arrest the attraction of the greater magnet, propose to explain the mysteries of our souls; or what remedy to substitute for the experience of renewed hearts? They have not succeeded with their own disciples; and they cannot satisfy the longing of the soul, or give peace to the weary. . . . The next generation will only remember their names to record their blindness.[650]

Society now-a-days abounds with men whose knowledge would be easily exhausted by two or three questions, and whose stock-arguments about the Bible are the most silly, shallow, and threadbare, but who pass as exceedingly clever and enlightened, with just a *soupcon* of mischief, on the ground of a weak infidelity. Not that their mental capacity or their moral character would entitle them to any influence whatever; and yet their trivialities too often have a damaging effect.[651]

If there is no such thing as a rose, why will you quarrel about its being either red or white, great or small, prickly or smooth? What is the good

---

649. OT, 140
650. Elijah, 213
651. True, 70

of attacking inspiration, or the fall, or miracles, or this or that book in the bible, if Jesus of Nazareth is not the Christ, the Son of the Living God? [652]

A SCEPTIC IS NOT one who has doubts and difficulties, but one who has them as his final state. Those twisted rocks and hills are not molten stuff, although they have passed through that stage, and so arrived at their present condition.[653]

Slavery

THE [LAW OF MOSES] begins, as assuredly none other ever did, not at the topmost but at the lowest rung of society. It declares in the first place the personal rights of such individuals as are in a state of dependence - male and female slaves . . . if slavery was still tolerated, as a thing existent, its real principle, that of making men chattels and property, was struck at the root, and the institution became, by its safeguards and provisions, quite other from what it has been among any nation, whether ancient or modern.[654]

BESIDES, JUDAISM FOUND SLAVERY as a social institution, intimately connected with the habits and war rights of the ancient world. To have isolated the Jews from this practice would have been almost impossible; but Judaism busied itself to mitigate, and, as much as possible, to abolish it.[655]

Society

THE DANGER IS ALL the greater, that this practice of calling evil good has almost become one of the conventionalities of society.[656]

    652. Tohu, 32
    653. Tohu, 55
    654. OT, 209
    655. Nation, 302
    656. Elijah, 45

Solomon

DAVID NAMED HIM, SYMBOLICALLY and prophetically, Solomon, "the peaceful:" the seal, the pledge, and the promise of peace. But God called him, and he was "Jedidiah," the Jehovah loved. Once more, then, the sunshine of god's favor had fallen upon David's household – yet was it, now and ever afterwards, the sunlight of autumn rather than that of summer; a sunlight, not of undimmed brightness, but amidst clouds of storm.[657]

THUS SOLOMON'S PRAYER [1 Kings 8] avoided alike the two extremes of unspiritual realism and of unreal spiritualism.[658]

Sorrows

MOST OF OUR SORROWS are only such because of our partial knowledge of them.[659]

Spiritual Warfare

OUR CHIEF DANGER LIES not in our enemies, but in our own use of carnal weapons, or in our distrust of His help and presence.[660]

FOR WHEN SATAN CANNOT otherwise oppose, he calls forth in us unbelieving doubts as to our aptitude or call for a work.[661]

ISRAEL MUST LEARN THAT the heathen nations were not only hostile *political* powers, opposing their progress, but that heathenism itself was in its nature antagonistic to the kingdom of God.[662]

---

657. OT, 542
658. OT, 606
659. Tohu, 62
660. Golden, 9
661. OT, 176
662. OT, 274

His Quotes

To us also has our Joshua given entrance into Canaan, and victory over our enemies – the world, the flesh, and the devil. We have *present* possession of the land. But, we do not yet hold all its cities, nor are our enemies exterminated. It needs on our part constant faith; there must be no compromise with the enemy, no tolerance of his spirit, no cessation of our warfare.[663]

The two most powerful instruments which the Enemy wields against the cause of God are ridicule and denial of God's truth.[664]

People will never want prudential motives for *not* doing that which is good, and Satan always has the best in such logic.[665]

Suffering

But as regards the earthly aspect of this "why" it is perhaps remarkable that such questions are more frequently put by strangers than by the sufferers themselves.[666]

The very thought that suffering was not *endurance*, but endurance *with a purpose* and under such direction, lifted it from the region of dull, weary, hopeless bearing into the sublime sphere of personal submission, so as thereby to be fitted for service and perfectness.[667]

Just as suffering awakes into fresh pain what in our body had previously been affected by disease, so old wounds of the spirit superficially healed over, will break out and smart anew.[668]

---

663. OT, 327
664. Elijah, 54
665. True, 67
666. Elijah, 121
667. True, 156
668. Rosenbaum, 95

Superstition

Anything, however indifferent, ceases to be indifferent if absolute value is attached to it, and they who practice it regard it not as indifferent, but as necessary, or most important. Superstition is to place a thing above its proper value, and above its proper place; it is misplaced religion, the putting a value upon things which they do not possess in themselves.[669]

Synagogue

The origin of the synagogue is lost in obscurity of tradition. Of course, like so many other institutions, it is traced by the Rabbis to the patriarchs.[670]

In point of fact, the attentive reader of the books of Ezra and Nehemiah will discover in the period after the return to Babylon the beginnings of the synagogue. Only quite rudimentary as yet, and chiefly for the purposes of instructing those who had come back ignorant and semi-heathenish – still, they formed a starting point.[671]

Talmud

Talmudism is in truth an exaggeration, or perhaps, as we should more correctly say, a caricature of the Old Testament . . . To this we must add the influence of the times and circumstances in which the Talmud was composed, and also the mental and moral idiosyncrasies of the various Rabbis, each straining his ingenuity to support an opinion, or to find an excuse for a special line of conduct, and each trying to outdo the other – and the origin of what forms the staple of most anti-Jewish charges will be readily understood. But, side by side with all this, we meet also with the most beautiful and even spiritual sayings, the outcome of the true Old

---

669. Elijah, 176
670. Sketches, 230
671. Sketches, 231

Testament spirit ... Neither sweeping praise nor sweeping blame can be the result of earnest impartial study of Rabbanism. It simply reflects the spirit of the people and of the times.[672]

BUT ISRAEL HAS ONE eminent work which she regards as the greatest literary *chef d'oeuvre* ever written; the possession of which, says a Jewish historian, ought to compensate all Hebrews for the loss of their ancestral country. And this work is the Talmud – a book which forms a kind of homestead for the Jewish mind, an intellectual and moral fatherland for a people who are exiles and aliens in all the nations of the earth.[673]

MOSES APPOINTED THE PRIESTS, the sons of Levi, as the religious teachers of Israel. The Talmud has ousted them altogether from their office.[674]

BUT THERE ARE IMPORTANT admissions, ascribed to Rabbis belonging to the Apostolic or Early Post-Apostolic age, which are at least negatively of great evidential value. Thus miracles on the part of Jesus seemed to be admitted, and they are not accounted for by delusion or imposture. However accounted for, we find the belief in the miraculous power of Jesus confirmed.[675]

WHILE ADMITTING THE TALMUDIC writings are utterly untrustworthy as regards historical accuracy, this much at least seems established from them, that miraculous power of healing was attributed to Jesus and to the early Christians; that their sacred writings – presumably in Aramaean – existed, were known, and circulated; that there was extensive religious communication between the disciples of Christ and the most eminent Teachers of the Law, and frequent, if not regular, discussions with them; and that many of the leaders of the Jewish world, and naturally many more of the people, were affected by the new movement.[676]

---

672. Watchman, August 1877, p. 142
673. Modern, 172
674. Modern, 189
675. Prophecy, 73
676. Prophecy, 86

THE TALMUD [IN APPLICATION of Isaiah 3:1] compares the Halacha to bread and the Hagada to water, because the later was even more frequently required, and was more refreshing than the former.[677]

The Temple

WHEN IT IS REMEMBERED that the building of the Temple preceded the legislation of Lycurgus in Sparta by about one hundred and twenty years; that of Solon in Athens by more than four hundred years; and the building of Rome by about two hundred and fifty years, it will be perceived that the kingdom of Solomon's presented the dim possibility of the intellectual, if not the political Empire of the world.[678]

THE TOTAL NUMBER OF [Temple builders] employed (160,000), though large, cannot be considered excessive, when compared, for example, with the 360,000 persons engaged for twenty years on the building of one pyramid.[679]

TRUE, IN ARCHITECTURAL SPLENDOR the second, as restored by Herod, far surpassed the first temple. But, unless faith had recognised in Jesus of Nazareth 'the Desire of all nations,' who should 'fill this house with glory' (Hag. 2:7), it would have been difficult to draw other than sad comparisons. Confessedly, the real elements of Temple-glory no longer existed. The Holy of Holies was quite empty, the ark of the covenant, with the cherubim, the tables of the law, the book of the covenant, Aaron's rod that budded, and the pot of manna, were no longer in the sanctuary. The fire that had descended from heaven upon the altar was extinct. What was far more solemn, the visible presence of God in the Shechinah was wanting.[680]

677. Nation, 322
678. OT, 546
679. OT, 593
680. Temple, 37

His Quotes

Tefillin

The very term used by the Rabbis for phylacteries – "Tephillin," prayer-fillets – is of comparatively modern origin, in so far as it does not occur in the Hebrew Old Testament. The Samaritans did not acknowledge them as of Mosaic obligation, any more than do the Karaite Jews, and there is, what seems to us, sufficient evidence, even from Rabbinical writings, that in the time of Christ phylacteries were not universally worn, nor yet by the priests while officiating in the Temple.[681]

But as for the value and importance in the eyes of the Rabbis, it were impossible to exaggerate it. They were reverenced as highly as the Scriptures, and, like them, might be rescued from the flames on a Sabbath., although not worn, as constituting "a burden!" it was said that Moses had received the law of their observance from God on Mount Sinai; that the "tephillin" were more sacred than the golden plate on the forehead of the high-priest, since its inscription embodied only once the sacred name of Jehovah, while the writing inside the "tephillin" contained it no less than twenty-three times; that the command of wearing them equaled all other commandments put together, with many other similar extravagances . . .

Before passing from this subject, it may be convenient to explain the meaning of the Greek term "phylacteries" for the "tephillin," and to illustrate its aptness. It is now almost generally admitted, that the real meaning of phylacteries is equivalent to amulets or charms. And as such the Rabbinists really regarded and treated them, however much they might otherwise have disclaimed all connection with heathen views.[682]

---

681. Sketches, 203
682. Sketches, 205

Temptation

To flee from temptations is already to have gained the victory over them; knowingly to expose ourselves to them is already to have been overcome, for it implies to a certain extent the consent of the heart.[683]

Tiberius

Tiberius is but a small town, and its walls and towers bear evidence of the terrible ravages caused by the earthquake of 1837. Not a solitary building remains of the ancient city, nothing in fact but heaps of stones, and some twenty or more granite columns. The present population is about two thousand, of which about half are Jews of the most sickly and squalid type. The Jewish quarter is in the middle of the town, where there are several synagogues and schools. A little to the north of this spot is a small Latin convent and church, built, according to tradition, on the very ground where the miraculous draught of fishes was landed after our Lord's resurrection.[684]

Titus (The Roman Emperor)

Nature and art seemed to have combined in favoring Titus. His face was handsome, and his figure, though not tall, was commanding . . . His licentiousness was famous even in dissoluble Rome.[685]

Tongue

The tongue which God had given only to praise Him had become a dangerous member – a circumstance which even its position within the twofold walls of cheeks and teeth indicated. [686]

683. Elisha, 200
684. Modern, 80
685. Nation, 90
686. Nation, 326

His Quotes

Tradition

ACCORDINGLY, SO IMPORTANT WAS tradition, that the greatest merit a Rabbi could claim was the strictest adherence to the traditions, which he had received from his teacher. Nor might one Sanhedrin annul, or set aside, the decrees of its predecessors. To such length did they go in this worship of the letter, that the great Hillel was actually wont to mispronounce a word, because his teacher before him had done so.[687]

Transfiguration

FEW, IF ANY, WOULD be so bold as to assert that the whole of this history had been invented by the three Apostles, who professed to have been its witnesses. Nor can any adequate motive be imagined for its invention. It could not have been intended to prepare the Jews for the Crucifixion of the Messiah, since it was to be kept a secret till after His resurrection; and, after the event, it could not have been necessary for the assurance of those who believed in the Resurrection, while to others it would carry no weight. Again, the special traits of this history are inconsistent with the theory of its invention. In a legend, the witnesses of such an event would not have been represented as scarcely awake, and not knowing what they said.[688]

Trials

IT IS A COMMON mistake to suppose that earnest religion and uprightness must necessarily be attended by success, even in this world. It is, indeed, true that God will not withhold any good thing from those whose Sun and Shield He is; but then success may not always be a good thing for them. Besides, God often tries the faith and patience of His people – and that is the meaning of many trials.[689]

687. LTJM, 68
688. LTJM, 542
689. OT, 105

To explain a trial would be to destroy its object, which is that of calling forth simple faith and implicit obedience. If we knew why the Lord sent this or that trial, it would thereby cease to be a trial either of faith or patience.[690]

It is marvelous how speedily not only the effects but almost the remembrance of former trials passes from us, when, in God's great mercy, we are transferred into new scenes and circumstances – new so far as concerns outward matters, but especially the moral atmosphere which we breathe.[691]

Trinity

Our theology is but Divine truth, presented in human form. Even that primal truth of Three Persons in the Godhead, or rather of their interrelation, is presented to us in a form adapted to the earthly and human. There is higher truth beyond it – only symbolised by the present mode of our apprehending it.[692]

Truth

For all proper defense of truth must aim after this positive result: more clearly to define, and more accurately to set forth, that which is certainly believed among us.[693]

We must ever distinguish between an antagonism which springs up by the side of truth and keeps peace with its progress, and mere denunciations which can only lead to political results, and have nothing of the religious in them. It may be truthful, it may be right, it may even be duty to denounce, if in room of what you sweep away you have some reality to offer. It can never be right or duty simply to denounce -to destroy without

---

690. Elisha, 156
691. Robbie, 104
692. Tohu, 58
693. Prophecy, vii

His Quotes

building; at least if the converse of error may not be mere negation but some positive truth.[694]

Types

IF ANYONE FAILED TO see in Isaac or in Joseph a personal type of Christ, he could not deny that the offering up of Isaac, or the selling of Joseph, and his making provision for the sustenance of his brethren, are typical of events in the history of our Lord.[695]

Unbelief

BUT MORE SAD AND discouraging by far than the direct opposition of the ungodly, is the unbelief and faintheartedness of God's own people.[696]

STRANGE THOUGH IT MAY appear, it is more pleasing to our unbelief to depend upon God for spiritual than for temporal things; far easier to believe in answers to things unseen than to those that are seen.[697]

ALL UNWILLINGNESS, WHETHER PRACTICAL or lurking in the heart, springs from unbelief.[698]

BREAD AND MEAT WOULD be given [to the children of Israel], both directly sent from God, yet both so given that, while unbelief was inexcusable, it should still be possible.[699]

THE WRONG OF OUR rebellion and unbelief is not turned into right by attempting the exact opposite. It is still the same spirit, which prompted

---

694. Reformers, 237
695. OT, 8
696. Golden, 21
697. Golden, 234
698. Golden, 283
699. OT, 195

the one, that influences the other. The obedience which is not of simple faith is of self-confidence, and only another kind of unbelief and self-righteousness.[700]

But, at bottom, the ground of despair and of rebellion, both on the part of the people and of Moses, was precisely the same. In both cases it was really unbelief of God. The people had looked upon Moses and not upon God as their leader into the land, and they had despaired. Moses looked at the people as they were in themselves, instead of thinking of God Who now sent them forward, secure in His promise, which he would assuredly fulfill.[701]

So we also, instead of immediately and almost instinctively resorting to God, too often forget Him till every other means has been exhausted, when we apply to Him rather from despair than from faith.[702]

Victory

How solemn to think of our responsibility as the representatives of the kingdom of God, with enemies watching on every side for our halting, and narrowly observing us! But herein also lies our comfort, that God cannot, under such circumstances, leave us to 'the will of our enemies.'[703]

If we have assurance of his presence, we shall be prepared to encounter any foe or to undertake any labour. What we need is full conviction. Firmly convinced that our sins are really forgiven, we have boldness of access unto God. Fully believing that none shall pluck us out of His hand, the spiritual contest is no longer uncertain, and need not be feared. Certain that the lord will give that which is good, the issue of future events is no longer doubtful, and we banish alike care and anxiety.[704]

700. OT, 247
701. OT, 258
702. OT, 780
703. Golden, 35
704. Elijah, 211

His Quotes

Moses fasted in the middle, Elijah at the end, Jesus at the beginning of his ministry. Moses fasted in the presence of God; Elijah alone; Jesus assaulted by the devil. Moses had been called up by God; Elijah had gone forth in the bitterness of his own spirit; Jesus was driven by the Spirit. Moses failed after his forty days' fast, when in indignation he cast the Tables of the law from him; Elijah failed before his forty days' fast; Jesus was assailed for forty days and endured the trial. Moses was angry against Israel; Elijah despaired of Israel; Jesus overcame for Israel.[705]

His Temptation and Victory have therefore a twofold aspect: the general human and the Messianic, and these two are closely connected. Hence we draw also this happy inference: in whatever Jesus overcame, we can overcome. Each victory which He has gained secures its fruits for us who are His disciples (and this alike objectively and subjectively). We walk in His foot-prints; we can ascend by the rock-hewn steps which His Agony has cut.[706]

Weakness

My weakness lies in what the world calls strength.[707]

Wisdom

It is a fallacy to suppose that age brings wisdom or knowledge. The lapse of time adds nothing to our potentiality, it only develops what is in us. At the age of sixty a man is either a perfect fool, or he ought to have a good deal of sense.[708]

---

705. LTJM, 205
706. LTJM, 205
707. Golden, 77
708. Tohu, 99

Woman

We need not wonder, although we take notice of it, that the position of woman in Israel should have been so different from that generally assigned to her in the East. A nation which counted among its historical personages a Miriam, a Deborah, and an Abigail – not to speak of other well-known figures – must have recognised the dignity of woman.[709]

Christianity has first raised woman to her proper position, not by giving her a new one, but by restoring and fully developing that assigned to her in the Old Testament.[710]

At the outset, we should here say, that even the Hebrew name for "woman," given her at creation (Gen 2:23), marked a wife as the companion of her husband, and his equal ("Ishah," a woman, from "Ish," a man).[711]

The ministry of woman to our blessed Lord, and in the Church, has almost become proverbial. Her position there marks really not a progress upon, but the full carrying out of, the Old Testament idea; or, to put the matter in another light, we ask no better than that any one who is acquainted with classical antiquity should compare what he reads of a Dorcas, of the mother of Mark, of Lydia, Priscilla, Phoebe, Lois, or Eunice, with what he knows of the noble women of Greece and Rome at that period.[712]

In general, the whole tendency of the Mosaic legislation, and even more explicitly that of later Rabbinical ordinances, was in the direction of recognising the rights of woman, with a scrupulousness which reached down even to the Jewish slave, and a delicacy that guarded her most sensitive feelings.[713]

709. OT, 835
710. LTJM, 705
711. Sketches, 95
712. Sketches, 131
713. Sketches, 132

His Quotes

A GOOD VOICE WAS the one qualification needful for a Levite. In the Second Temple female singers seem at one time to have been employed (Ezra 2:65; Neh. 7:67)[714]

Words

WORDS ARE WINGED MESSENGERS of peace or of war, of life or of death; and it is far better, difficult as to some it may seem, to be silent than to speak, when such speaking is in the service of the devil, rather than of God.[715]

The World

VIEWS ON THE PERFECTIBILITY of the world are prone to lead us to fellowship with the world, and to undue conformity to its enjoyments. Let us remember that we are 'in a strange land,' where the language of Canaan is not spoken, and the authority of its king not owned.[716]

IN MEASURE AS WE live in the world to come has this world lost its power over us.[717]

THE WORLD DOES NOT ask us to surrender religion; it only opposes earnest, genuine religion.[718]

WE ARE AFRAID TO appear singular; we wish to occupy our proper place; we must be like our neighbours; our children, our connections, our business requires conformity to the world. But if, indeed, spiritual things have been a reality to us; if we have fled for refuge to the hope set before us in the Gospel; if we have been purchased with the precious Blood of Jesus, if we have laid up our treasures in Heaven – let us consider and see what we

714. Temple, 53
715. Elijah, 20
716. Golden, 72
717. Golden, 138
718. Elisha, 52

are doing when thus identifying ourselves with the world, as we go to the ballroom or the theatre.[719]

FAITH IN GOD MAKES us optimists: experience of the world and of men, pessimists. Can we be both at the same time? Yes, by renouncing the world.[720]

VIEWED ABSTRACTLY, THERE IS nothing unlawful in any occupation or trade – the danger lies in the unchristian manner of carrying it on, or in the abuse of it. Still, some occupations are in themselves more perilous than others; only sin, or what directly ministers to it, is contrary to the Word of God . . . Thus the tailor may not minister to the vanity of his customers; the vintner must be strictly honest, nor may he entertain more than travelers.[721]

Worship

THERE IS A VAST difference between *worship* and *service*. We *serve* in *our own houses*, having worshipped him in *His* house. Service is work, and work for Him where *He* places us, not where we place ourselves.[722]

Zeal

FOR, THE ZEAL OF those whose religion is not spiritual often exceeds that of the children of God. The sectarian is generally far more zealous for his Shibboleth than the child of God against the common enemies of Israel, or for Israel's God. The reason is, that his party zeal constitutes the sum and substance of his religion. If it be taken from him, nothing else is left.[723]

---

719. Elisha, 63
720. Tohu, 126
721. Reformers, 244
722. Elisha, 6
723. Elisha, 37

Appendix A

Whose is Thine Heart?

Here is the entire sermon which Edersheim gave on March 30, 1851. It was delivered to the *Foreign Conference and Evangelization Committee* at the *Reading and Committee Rooms,* 47 Leicester Square. In his preface he says it is "meant to be a plain statement of what is held and cherished as the truth," directed toward "all those (especially the young persons) who, while professing to be Christians, are still strangers to the power of the gospel." It is an impassioned plea to give one's heart to God, based on Proverbs 23:26.

∼

You have, no doubt, my brethren, heard of the fact that, when two harps or other musical instruments are strung to the same key-note, the vibration of the chord in one instrument, calls forth spontaneously a similar vibration in the corresponding chord of the other instrument. To mount in the scale of comparison – Do not we in some measure observe the same in ourselves? How often do we feel as if a look, a word, an expression, were like the vibration of a chord calling forth a similar vibration within us? Men call this sympathy. In truth, there seems to be a general law at the basis of this, and similar correspondences of which our world is full, be they between the outward object and the eye, or the sound and the ear; or, thought and thought, feeling and fellow-feeling – I say a law of correspondence whether in the unison or the harmony, (for in both there is correspondence), which in its unity points to adaptation, in adaptation to purpose, and, in purpose, to mind. Thence we gather one of the strongest and most convincing proofs, that all that we see around us is the workmanship of "the God of all the earth."

Appendix A

This, for want of a better name, we might designate as proof *external*. But, to our mind, a yet stronger evidence, and not of observation and instruction, but we would almost say of intuition, is that furnished by *proof internal* in the correspondence, whether of unison or harmony, between the Bible and our inner man.

The word of God – we feel it – brings before us what meets the wants of our soul, what finds an echo in the chord deepest in our very heart of hearts; in it we have a note, which, finding its note in the heart of every one "that hath ears to hear;" – and of all passages, of all expressions in all scripture, none perhaps more so than the text chosen for meditation.

Look around you my brethren; alas! How much grief, how much sorrow, nay, making abstraction of *positive* grief and sorrow, what a total absence, and felt-want of comfort and joy! How speedily do all objects fade, and with them how speedily do our affections and hearts, set upon these objects, wither! But in Jesus Christ, "the same yesterday, to day, and for ever," our deepest wants find not only satisfaction, but lasting, ay, and *everlasting* satisfaction! The edifice of our hope and joy may be built not only upon *a* rock, but upon Thee Rock of Ages; for the world addressed to us, and that from Jehovah's lips, is "My son, give *me* thine heart."

In calling your attention to this text, you will easily understand that we must confine ourselves to a few truths contained in it, which we shall arrange, for order and distinction's sake, under these two heads:

First, the meaning of our text. Secondly, it's practical bearing.

First, then, let us meditate on the meaning of the text. False religion, of whatever kind, may, we think, be arranged under one of these three heads – it is either the religion of mere intellect; or that of base fear; or, lastly, that of tradition and custom. But, in contradistinction thereto, our test brings before us three leading features of true religion – features not only distinctive from, but opposed to those previously traced. First, as to its seat, we have it – "My son, give me thine *heart*." Secondly, as to its chief object: but as the chief object is always the chief motive also, if in false religion the chief motive was base fear, in true religion the chief object, and hence the chief motive, is essentially different – it is no more self, but God – "My son, give *me* thine heart." Lastly, in its realisation, true religion is characterized by liberty and choice, in opposition to mere habit; - "*Give me thine heart.*"

The first difference that we notice is in the *seat* of true religion. In opposition to the religion of mere intellect, the Gospel calls upon us – "My son, give me thine *heart*."

What most strikes and chills the observer in men and their ways, is their heartlessness. Young and inexperienced persons, who see the world through the glass of their fancy, do not expect such discoveries, and, in the ardour of their own feeling, little dream that they ever may be influenced by the same motives – that they may be gliding along the same stream which they cannot but see gradually carrying down their neighbour's bark. But ah! Painful experience will teach that "all seek their own;" and as every new discovery – as every new disappointment, saps the foundation of his dreams, man either joins the crowd, or is buried in the ruins.

This heartlessness, so clearly and unmistakably written on the ways of the world, is, indeed, but the necessary expression of original sin, of original apostasy from God, and the establishment of self in the room and place of the Lord. Selfishness, the fundamental principal, the mainspring of every sin, it is, to which heartlessness stands so closely allied. Twin-daughters of hell; the one grasping, the other repelling; the one attracting, the other destroying; the one alluring, the other mocking; each presupposes and supplements the other. Another circumstance tending to supply fuel to the flame of selfishness, in its characteristic manifestation of heartlessness, is the real and felt insufficiency of what this world offers to our soul's wants. For as every new disappointment shuts up one walk after the other, one prospect after the other, stone is added to stone in that high and impenetrable wall which surrounds the heart, till at last every access, every prospect, is closed up – man lives, and *consciously* lives, for self, and self alone. This is the full development of sin.

Specially noticeable is this feature in its religious bearing. In fact heartlessness, in a more extended sense, constitutes the irreligious, and characterises the mere profession, of men. The heart is set on self; they love not the ways of the Lord, they care not for them, they seek not nor desire the blessed realities of an unseen and eternal world; they will not have this man reign in and over them; "God is not in all their thoughts;" their heart is on other things – on all things, nay on *no* things; self is their all and in all. This is the key to the unwillingness of men to listen to the truth, the explanation of the reception they gave it; they see no beauty in Him that they should desire Him. Or, on the other hand, notice the

Appendix A

same feature in the religion of the unconverted man. You may disarm him, you may silence him, you may bring him to acknowledge certain facts, to forego certain sins, and to conform to certain practices, but you cannot reach his heart. Hence, whether in the world or the professing Church – whether in his family or in his closet – going to the house of God, listening to His Word, or in conversation about religious matters, reading the Bible, yea, in prayer, meditation, humiliation, aspiration – the same mark of the curse is imprinted everywhere – *his heart is not there*. The heart, the seat of the affections, is unmoved, cold, dead, hard as the nether millstone. But how different, beloved, when Christ is received! How different when this is realized – "My son give me thine heart!" The Gospel, you will observe, addresses itself to the heart, it does not simply say, Acknowledge – make a godly profession; but it says, primarily and chiefly, "My son, give *me thine heart.*" It addresses itself to the heart, with its invitations, with its promises, with its blessings, with its comforts, with its hopes, with its joys. And as it addressed itself to the heart, so it first opens the heart; and as it opens the heart, so it claims the whole heart; and as it claims the whole heart, so it purifies the heart; and as it purifies the heart, so it renews the heart; and as it renews the heart, so it sanctifies the heart; and as it sanctifies the heart, so it satisfies the heart, aye, and blesseth it with *everlasting* blessings – blessings which have no end – blessings which, like a chain, go on from link to link to all eternity. "My son, give me thine *heart.*" Christianity, the religion of the Gospel, is pre-eminently a religion *for the heart*, a religion *of the heart*, and a religion *in the heart*. It claims the heart, it dwells in the heart, it satisfies the heart.

So far, then, for the first leading feature in the text, which distinguisheth true religion from that of mere intellect. We now come to the second difference – in the motive and object. The chief object and the chief motive, we repeat, are always identical. The chief object of false religion, then, being fear, the chief object it has in view is the removal of this fear – that is, a certain ease of mind here, and security from punishment hereafter. But in opposition to this, our text points to the chief motive, and hence the chief object, of true religion, as Jehovah God – "My son, give *me* thine eart."

You will farther agree, that if, as we said above, true religion is that of the heart, and the heart must be given to an object, this object can not be anything abstract – it must be something living, real, personal. Hence it is not said, "My son, give thine heart to a truth," nor "to a system of truths." No, the warm heart that beats within us must have a living object; it cannot deal with abstractions. The mind deals with abstractions, the heart with living realities. Hence the object which is set before the heart is not a truth, nor a system of truths, but He who is the truth. "Give *me* thine heart." It is not with any *it* you are brought in contact in true religion; it is with God *himself*.

But to proceed: if the heart is to be given to God, one thing seems requisite – that we see his beauty and his excellency, and that we understand and feel that we may have possession and property in him. It is impossible in the full sense to give the heart to any object, unless, on the one hand, we behold, we feel, its beauty and excellency; and, on the other, understand that we may have possession therein, and be blessed in such possession. Hence, in order to give our heart to God, there must be a revelation on His part of beauty and excellency, a shining forth of His splendour, a revelation of His majesty. Yes, my brethren, there must be that which the natural mind has never perceived – that which the natural heart has never felt – which eyes that have not been opened by God's own hand have never beheld: there must be a manifestation of Him as Jehovah God. Ah! We know these are words which have no meaning for the unconverted; expressions which find no sympathy in their hearts; for these things are spiritually discerned, and the carnal mind and the carnal heart are equally strangers to them. But those who, having first been humbled, emptied, and made to long for Him, and Him alone, to whom He has spoken – not as professors fancy they hear His voice – whom He Himself has raised up, whose eyes He has opened, to whom He reveals Himself in His secret place, in His beauty and excellency, cast away mere notions and bare speculations – they understand His claims – they feel the unspeakable bliss of His call – "My son, give *me* thine heart."

We hasten to add, however, that this manifestation of God is found in Christ alone; and if God's beauty and excellency must be seen and felt before we can give Him our hearts, it follows that we must come to Jesus; as it is in Christ that God reveals Himself and shines forth. The mind that does not look to God in Christ cannot see Him at all. Many there are who see no beauty or excellency in Him. The ground thereof is, that, not looking to Christ, they do not see God, but only their own speculation, the reflection of their own minds. Hence also the gods of nature, the idols of unconverted persons – are so like themselves. Only when our eye is fixed on Jesus we *see* God; but then also we behold, we realise His beauty and

Appendix A

His excellency. If we look to Christ as He is held out in the word of God, in the promises, in the prophecies, oh! The faithfulness, the kindness, the mercy, of God! - If we look to Christ as we see Him born, as we see Him wrapped in swaddling clothes laid in the manger – if we look to Christ as we see Him in humiliation, when He came to fulfill the demands of a holy and just God, when we see the father so loved the world that He did not spare His only begotten son – when we see Christ agonizing in the garden – when we see Him sweating great drops of blood – when we see Him emptying the bitter cup to the very dregs – when we see Him led forth, mocked, spat upon, scourged, crucified between two malefactors – ah! when we see the veil of the temple rent, yea, and the graves open – when we see Christ rising to the right hand of God, and there sitting and making intercession for us, and, in Christ, full satisfaction and reconciliation made, and access opened, gifts received for the rebellious, grace, victory, triumph! –ah! if we come ourselves to the risen, gracious Saviour, who seeketh and saveth the lost – if by faith we lay hold on Him – if we drew out of his fullness and cleave to Him – what ineffably glorious views will we then have of the great *"I am, that I am!"* And while rejoicing that this "God is our God," yea, "our Father," we shall adore and praise Jehovah's holiness, justice, truth, faithfulness, kindness, mercy, love and grace. The whole splendour of Divine beauty, as it were, beams forth in the Sun of Righteousness, shedding its light and life and peace everywhere around, and illuminating the darkness of this world. Then – yea, on Calvary, my brethren – we can in some measure understand, feel, realise, reciprocate it – "My son, give *me* thine *heart.*"

But there is a third feature in true religion which we must notice – its realisation. It is not, my friends, a religion of formalism, nor of want and custom: it is, "My son, give me *thine* heart." And indeed, brethren, if you have so far followed and sympathized with us, you will understand that this surrender of the heart must be *free*, in the truest sense of the word – a *gift*. But a difficulty may here occur to some minds. Does not the idea of giving our heart destroy the view we formerly endeavoured to establish, of the necessity of the enlightenment of the mind and the quickening of the heart, connected with the revelation the Lord makes of Himself in Christ? Do the idea of a personal and free surrender, and that of the necessity of the work of God in us, not contradict each other? We answer, the contrary is the case. Listen to the Psalmist – "Thy people shall be willing in the day of thy power." Literally translated – "Thy people shall be free-will offerings in the day of thy power;" meaning – "Thy people shall bring themselves free-will sacrifices when thy power is seen and felt." And farther, if it be true that the heart of man is naturally selfish, "deceitful above all things, and desperately wicked" – if yours is to be a gift of the heart, a surrender of yourselves to God, does not this furnish you with the strongest proof of the necessity of the working of Divine grace, to make you *willing* thus to surrender? We grant it, a man is not forced – he gives himself willingly, freely, a "free-will offering" unto God, but that he may do so, the Spirit of God must first make him one of the "willing people;" for it is He that "works both to will and to do of his good pleasure." Just because it is not the bare, barren acknowledgement of the mind, the giving in of an intellect, that is silenced in all its objections – because it is the outflowing and outgoing of a heart, the streams of the heart having formerly flowed in a different direction – it presupposes of necessity a hand that stemmed these waters, and turned them into a different channel; it calls of necessity for Jehovah's working mightily in us, in order that we may now give ourselves unto Him. But let us also understand distinctly what is implied, at least to some extent, in the word "give."

There are two truths, methinks, pointed at in it. The first evidently is the call to *surrender* – "My son, *give*:" the second seems to imply not only a giving up, but also a reception of something else – a setting the affections on something different. When God calls upon me – "My son *give* me *thine heart*," he calls us to cast away all other things; and again, to receive also something else, something new, something higher, something better – even Jehovah the living God himself – "My son, give *me* thine heart." Our text thus embodies what the Apostle Paul expresses in a different way – "Yea, doubtless, I count all things but loss ('give') *for the excellency of the knowledge of Christ Jesus*" ("My son, *give* me *thine heart*"). Thus, then, when moved by the eternal Spirit of God, who reveals the beauty and excellency of Jehovah, His claims, and the blessedness of possession in Him, the soul surrenders willingly and freely everything else, all things are counted as loss for the "pearl of great price." The soul now, henceforth, and for ever, closes with Christ as its "all and in all" – turns to Him as "chiefest among ten thousand" – feels and realises that He is precious indeed. Now the affections are set on things on high, where *He* sitteth at the right hand of God; now the soul presses forward to that mark which is set before us in the Gospel; now he must "count all things but loss," that he may win Christ, and be found in Him, not having his own righteousness

Appendix A

which is by faith. "My son, give." Leave what thou hadst before; put off the rags; cast them off. Thou art called to "an inheritance incorruptible, undefiled, and that fadeth not away." Behold *me* thy possession, thy portion of thy cup, thine inheritance forever." *"Give me thine heart."*

So far then, brethren, for a theological view of our text. Let us now consider its practical bearing. Notice here, in the first place, the Lord's claim on us, "*my son* give me thine heart."

The Lord comes to thee, my brother, to thee, my sister. He claims thee for Himself. This claim is a claim of love: "My *son*, give me thine heart. I have a right to it, "My son" (I am thy God). I love thee, my *son* (I am thy Father). Long hast thou neglected, long hast thou forgotten, long hast thou forsaken me; yet I wait to be gracious unto thee. In my house there is bread enough and to spare. Return, O prodigal! There is in me a Father's heart that yearns after thee; there is with me a Father's provision ready to be vouchsafed unto thee; a Father's blessing ready to be poured out on thee; there is in me a Father's love, ready to make thee blessed in time and eternity. *Thou art mine.* If thou turnest away, it is an apostasy, it is in sin, it is in rebellion. I *claim thee* as mine. I knock at the door of thine heart; I come very near to thee; I spread forth my hand unto thee, "my son!" Canst thou resist the voice of him that speaketh? – the offended Judge, the righteous Lawgiver, the Great, the holy One of Israel, who inhabiteth the praises of eternity – He in whose dread presence thou shalt soon have to appear – it is even He who pleads with thee – *"My son, give me thine heart."*

Notice, further, the invitation. "Give me thine heart." Who is it that asks? Of whom does he ask? Who does he ask? When does he ask? How does he ask? All these questions speak volumes. It is God that asks it of *thee*, of every one amongst us. God asks thee to *give* it, not to be willing to give it on a future occasion, not to resolve to give it, but to give it *now*; He asks thee to give it *as it is*; He asks thee to give it that He might bless it, that He may purify it, that He may dwell in it, that He may sanctify it, that He may glorify Himself in it, that He may transform thee into His own image. Give it to Him: freely surrender it, freely yield it up an offering unto the Lord. Let thine affections be set on Him; Let thy soul's desire go out after Him. The Lord invites thee, "Give me thine heart."

But suppose this invitation listened to, suppose this behest obeyed, and the heart given. Look for a moment at the consequences thereof. Henceforth, we are no more our own, we are no more the world's, we no more belong to any individual creature, or to all creatures. We are free! See the bondage of the children of men; they have many masters. God calls *you to liberty*. Be no more thy own – belong no more to any creature: be mine – be free!" But, if so, thy thoughts, thy desires, thy words, thy ways, must be no more thine own. As long as thine heart is thine own, so will all these be; but if thou art His property, if He dwelleth in thee – then thou art His, in the strictest sense of the word, with all the privileges and duties it implies – His own. Thou belongest to God. He holds possession of the heart; He reigns there; He dwells there. But never forget that the person to whom thou art called to give thy heart is God; and that, if really His, He now reigns in thee, and He is God not only over, but in thee, and that with thine own consent. Thy thoughts are now to be His, thy desires, thy ways, are His; and all this heartily, not grudgingly: yea, it is the object, end, and aim, of all thy desires that it should be so. Thy heart is given to the Lord, and He reigns in thee. Nor is thy consent grudgingly extracted; but He reigns with thy full approbation – with all thy desires. Thou desirest, thou lovest to be His.

Suppose a man thus heartily giving himself to God: how different is he from the men of the world. How different in all his transactions! He will long to be away from the men of the world – from the joys of the world; he will feel himself a stranger in the midst of them: it will not be a sacrifice to him when he is called upon to separate himself from it – or to bare witness for God in the midst of scorners and scoffers – or when he was publicly to confess that he is the Lord's servant. He desires that it should be so he has given his heart to God, and he feels that the Lord dwells in and reigns over his heart. In trials he feels that it is God's hand, and he willingly consents to God's government. He is no more his enemy, he is no more murmuring and gainsaying; he is willingly falling into the plan of God, if I may use such an expression; he goes along with the government of God willingly and heartily; he does not feel as if he was wronged or injured; he does not feel as if he was called upon to give up something near and dear to himself; he feels that the Lord's ways are ways of pleasantness – God is his king, and that with his full consent. He not only bows because he must bow; he is not only silent because he must be silent; he not only acquiesces because he must acquiesce; he not only bends his neck to the yoke because he must bend his neck to the yoke. The great, the leading, the marked characteristic, is different – in all that he does in the service of God he is hearty. It is not grudgingly that he gives to the cause of Christ, that he goes to the house of God, that he listens to the word of God, it is not grudgingly that he bends his knee in prayer, willing to escape it if he could, but obliged for conscience' sake to do so; it is not reluctantly that he pleads the cause of Christ with the unconverted, and displays the banner of truth and righteousness. He delights in these things – they are his joy and his comfort. He has given his heart to God, and he feels that all this is too little. His great desire, his leading thought is, Oh! That the Lord was more exalted, more glorified – that I was more His! – "Thy kingdom come; Thy will be done in earth, *as it is done in heaven.*"

You may suppose *that* man in the different walks of usefulness; you may suppose him in the Sabbath-school, in missionary labour, in the church of the living God, in his business, in the world, in his family, in different circumstances and relations – one thing remains unchanged – God in Christ is all in all; "the chiefest among ten thousand, and altogether lovely." How many of my hearers are hearty in their religion? How many of you, my brethren, have given your hearts to God? In your duties – in your Sabbath-school teaching – in your profession, in your families, in your business – in your joys, in your trials – say, is God in all your thoughts? yet our text says, "My son, give me thine heart."

Here, also, my friends, we have some precious helps, especially the younger among us. We find in the text some encouragement to choose this way of the Lord; of which a few only can be mentioned. In the measure that the heart is given to God, you have safety from temptation, because the sting of temptation is taken away. For what is the sting of temptation, indeed what is it that constitutes temptation but the heart's consent? You will find this in the Epistle of James, 1:13,14 – "Let no man say when he is tempted, I am tempted of God, for God cannot be tempted with evil, neither tempteth he any man. But every man is tempted" – when? – "when he is drawn away of his own lust." Not until the heart's consent is given does it become temptation. Before it was trial; now it becomes temptation. But if the heart is given to God, its consent can not be given to these things; the affections are set upon different things; their surrender is no sacrifice; for the Lord is espoused by the heart. He is owned, He is loved, He is desired. Thus temptation loses its sting – that which constitutes its temptation.

Again: you have in the text a direction in all difficulties, "My son, give me thine heart." "Seek first the kingdom of God and his righteousness." If I am in difficulty and doubt – if I know not whither to turn – if I am perplexed, what shall I do? My soul, call upon the Lord. "Give me thine heart," He says to me. "Thy face, Lord, will I seek." Is the soul's answer I not whither to turn – I am anxious to find my way, yet bewildered, amazed, in darkness, doubt and difficulty. Hear the voice of the Lord – "My son, give me thine heart." Doubts and difficulties now vanish for the heart is given to God. Here then you have also direction, comfort, and solution of all difficulty.

Again: You have a new end and aim in life. As long as the end and aim of your life is self, there must be antagonistic forces meeting and clashing with each other. Look at the world: it is at enmity with itself. There is no truth more real, more self evident, than this: hateful, hating one another." Every individual unconverted man is a fortress garrisoned by self, and held for self; and it is the law in that fortress that everything must be subject to self. Selfishness demands the gratification of self – the subjection of everything to self. This garrison, this citadel, meets with another garrison – another equally opposing host, whose end, aim, and object, must be the same – to subject the first. So that a selfish world must be in a constant enmity. Now you are to be turned in a different direction. However the Church is like a flock following one shepherd, and its numbers no more hateful and hating one another. You will find this contrast beautifully described in Titus 3:3. Now there is a new direction; now there is a new road open – now a new end, aim, and object of life set before us – even Jehovah God and His glory. And amongst ourselves we are no more enemies, but fellow workers, pilgrims on the same road, following the same Master, holding the same truth, filled with the same hope, animated by the same comfort, having before us the same end – a brotherhood, a living temple – Jesus Christ himself being the chief cornerstone of that building, the Head of that Church, and God its Father.

So also, the text sets before us hopes, joys, and comforts, (as we have already hinted) – opens up a possession and an inheritance incorruptible, undefiled, and that fadeth not away. It gives us comfort not only in this life, but in death – opening before us the blessed realities of an unseen world; and assuring us that what now we have believed we shall then see; what now we have prayed we shall then praise for; unlocking the pearly gates of heaven, disclosing to us green pastures, and the quiet waters with the Lamb in the midst to lead and feed His people. Every other comfort,

Appendix A

hope, or joy, has no reality, for it wants stability – it wants character. Here then you have an everlasting hope, "good home through grace."

Such are a few of the considerations we might have dwelt upon, had time allowed, to show that the way of the Gospel is the way of pleasantness, and the invitation, if obeyed – the call, if listened to, in truth comforts and makes happy. We might, in conclusion, have spoken of the evidence by which to judge whether we are the children of God. If we have given our hearts to Him, we must have evidence of it. And let this one only be mentioned that if we are His sons we have not only given our hearts to Him, but we are giving them, for the religion of the Bible knows no past, but only the present tense.

In conclusion, we will only say that this text should be looked upon by the two classes of our hearers from a different point of view. The unconverted amongst us must look upon it as a call – a loud and solemn call. Brethren, God in His providence, God in His power, God by His message, God by His grace, says to each and all of you – "awake, sinner, careless, heartless, cold-harded, dead sinner – awake! My son, give me thine heart. Stand no longer far from me. Give me thy soul, thy affections – let them go out towards me." Brethren, no preparation is required – no time should be lost – no other object should be taken up. This is *the one thing needful* – even that you and I give our hearts unto God; and now every one of us is called upon – "my son, give me thine heart."

Again: To God's people amongst you we would say, let it be taken as the direction for your lives. Let it be your watchword. Keep your heart – keep the issues of it; let it be kept for God, and Go alone. Ah! dearly beloved, if any awakened sinner, or any backslider, or any who doubts, hesitates or fears, were but realising it, and obeying it, how blessed would he be! The Lord is waiting to be gracious. Look not to self; seek not thine own strength; but give thy heart to God in Christ. Cast thyself upon Him; embrace Him, as it were; take Him as thine all in all; cleave to Him, let Him be thy God, thy King. And as thou leavest this house, leave it with this holy resolution; and as thou enterest in the world again, enter it with this blessed purpose; and as thou goest to thy avocations, let this avow accompany thee; and as thou returnest to thy family, let this call follow thee, and as thou bendest thy knee, or openest thy Bible, let this voice still ring in thine ears, in thy conscience, in the heart – "My son, give me thine heart." Amen.

Appendix B

From Grey to Dawn

In the periodical *The Scattered Nation*, Alfred Edersheim serialized a work of historical fiction called, *From Grey to Dawn: A Tale of Jewish Life in the Time of Christ.* The main character is Marcos, a young Alexandrian Jew who makes the trip to Jerusalem to celebrate Passover in approximately the year 30 AD. He is disenchanted with the Greek philosophy which has greatly influenced the Judaism of his homeland. At the same time, he dislikes the overly legal developments of the Pharasaic tradition in Jerusalem. He is proud to be a Jew, although he is not fully clear on what that means. On the journey, he has encounters with various types of people, and he learns about a certain preacher from Nazareth who was gaining quite a following. Many were even saying that he was the long awaited Anointed One – the Messiah. But, what exactly did that mean? The following quotes are first-person accounts of these fictionalized characters. Marcos begins his story with the following words:

> *Am I wrong in supposing that every one makes his first start in life, or undertakes his first great journey, with indefinite expectations of a something new and great to be attained? Am I to make wonderful discoveries, like those dreamed of by the Platonists in our museum; or to meet great disappointments, and come home a confirmed old Stoic? Best, as uncle Jochanan says, to keep mind and heart open, to judge nothing hastily, and to be prepared for great changes in my views. And so I have resolved to note down, so far as I can, truthfully, my impressions, and to record events as they occur. And here is the commencement of it!*

Responding to the philosophy of a Greek friend he meets along the way, Marcos writes in his diary:

> *According to his own account he worships the true, the beautiful, and the good, wherever he can find it. He believes in everything and in no one thing. The gods are the ideas of the Divine presented in a*

> *concrete form, and adapted to the capacity of the vulgar. The true is the everlasting, the beautiful is the overcharming, and the good is the ever-desirable: an ideal which we must always pursue, but can never hope to attain. This is the Divine, and the Divine is in life. But to the question, what is the true, and what the good, his philosophy can give meaning at different times and different persons.*[1]

Similarly, the religion of his own people – both in Jerusalem and in his native Alexandria – raised questions in his mind. In another conversation, he explained:

> *For, by nationality, I, of course, always was a Jew, and do not care to be anything else. With such a history as ours, the prejudices of the vulgar and the persecutions of the Gentiles would only make me, if possible, more intensely Hebrew . . . But I tell you frankly, if Rabbanism were Judaism, I could not be a Jew. I would remain one nationally, and observe our great national feasts – at least so long as I could – but that would be all. And I cannot believe that any generous mind, unless from earliest thinking, sicklied by such an atmosphere, could feel otherwise than I. As for our Alexandrian Jewish philosophy, it is simply an affectation and an untruth. It is neither philosophy nor Judaism. It tries to be both, and perverts what is plainly intended in quite another sense, by a wretched system of mystification, into the jargon of philosophy.*[2]

Still later, Marcos meets a relative upon arriving in Hebron, the ancient city just outside of Jerusalem. He is not at ease with himself, as he wrestles with tradition, the scriptures and a future for the Jewish people.

> *I mean, that I can understand and glory in our past – in our law, in our prophets, in our history, in our Temple. But I cannot understand our present, and still less our future, viewing it in the light of the present. And yet if our past be all – if there is no future to unfold and to apply it; if the narrow present is to become only narrower, than even our past loses its meaning, or much of it. It is like a broken story, like buds that become not flowers, like – like the wishes of my heart.*[3]

Marcos meets another relative, his uncle Isaac, who was a rabbi living near Jerusalem. Rabbi Isaac began to tell him of the man from Nazareth

1. January 1, 1869
2. March, 1, 1869, p. 63
3. May 1, 1869, p. 116

– who was expected to attend this very Passover celebration in Jerusalem. Rabbi Isaac spoke in hushed tones, as it was in some circles already scandalous to mention his name. The events began some thirty years ago with a unique family. Rabbi Isaac continued:

> *They were said to be humble tradespeople from Galilee. When our sages saw them, they sneered with contempt, for they regard all Galileans as but little differing from Gentiles or publicans. Yet some who know their history, told that the youth Himself was born in Bethlehem, about the time of the general slaughter of its infants had taken place, and, besides, that He was of the royal line of David. They also declared, that he had been the only child who had escaped that massacre, by the secret flight of his parents.*[4]

Marcos and Rabbi Isaac talked late into the night. The old man was becoming more and more convinced that the times of the prophecies from the ancient Scriptures were now at hand. And that they centered around this man from Nazareth. Even his birth was a special event. Isaac recalled what happened some three decades earlier which they were later told (by some eye-witness shepherds) was the arrival a special king.

> *It was late in the season, but the sky was clear and starlit. We were parting at the door of this chamber, when your uncle [Jochanan], exclaimed, "Look, Bethlehem is in flames!" We rushed to the roof, but it was not fire we saw, only the whole of the plain seemed for a short time bathed in light. As we bent forward into the still night, our senses almost preternaturally quickened, it was as if borne on the breeze we caught strange notes, like those of the Temple, when the white-robed Levites in full choir intone their Hallelujah, and yet quite other than that. The sounds, if real sounds they were, died out, and tho light faded away, but we stood as entranced, our hearts filled with an emotion, which I had never before felt, and which I could not describe.*[5]

Approximately twelve years after that, Rabbi Isaac was in the Temple and saw a youth who possessed remarkable wisdom. It was surely the same one who had been born in Bethlehem.

> *But a most unusual sight also presented itself. A crowd of eager listeners and students surrounded a slim youth. There was no beauty in Him, but His every feature and look seemed to sink deep into your*

---

4. May 1, 1869, p. 143
5. May 1, 1869, p. 118

Appendix B

> heart, and to draw you with an irresistible power of mingled love and reverence. And yet He evidently belonged to the lower classes. But judge, what influence and manner his bearing must have had upon our Rabbis, when they would allow a stranger child to question them. While life lasts, I never can forget the scene. There was no trace of haste nor excitement about the youth. Most modestly He listened to the doctors, yet even when silent, he spake. It was not merely that his presence seemed to caste a halo around, but the questions which he put were really not questions but answers, and more than that – they seemed to give a new direction to every discussion. For some time I stood, hearing nothing but that voice, and seeing nothing but that Presence. When I looked from Him to our sages, I noticed how the cold grey eyes of the president fell before him; how quiet and humbled the proudest of them seemed, while here and there a flush stole over a withered face, or a tear rolled down a furrowed cheek. It was all about the law and the prophets, and the Passover, and the sacrifices, and the Temple, and the God of our fathers, of whom, with deep reverence, yet like one familiar with Him, he always spake as our Father. There was no contest of logical ingenuity that day, no vain glorious display, nor foolish quibbling, such as so often disgraces the teachings of our leaders. All was quiet and solemn, as if all had felt that we were about our Father's business.[6]

This talk gave young Marcos much to think about. The next day he continued to meet other characters, and even begins to fall in love with a young woman. Here, Edersheim displays the sensibilities of his own time. For, as much as he immerses the story in first century Jewish customs, this part of the drama almost has the feel of a Victorian Novel. Another person we meet is a Centurion (Roman Guard) in Galilee who had become a follower of the God of Abraham. He even built a Synagogue for the Jewish people (this is an obvious reference to Luke 7). When asked why he believed in God, and what God's purpose for gentiles was, the centurion said the following.

> I mean, that God called Israel for one purpose, and for another allowed us Gentiles to follow our own course. They received and held the revelation of God till the world should be ripe for its spread, then the narrow form in which the Jews kept the truth was to be enlarged till it would embrace all mankind. On our part we have been taught what poetry, the arts, science, and power, can achieve for man and what it cannot attain. And now we have learned our wants and our

---

6. May 1, 1869, p. 119

> incapacity of the Divine; yet what we have achieved – our learning, our civilisation, our one empire, and our one language – the noble Greek! – all these are now ready prepared as the means for the advancement of that Divine truth which is to give to all mankind true liberty, peace and virtue, and to teach each of us that we have a Father in heaven and a saviour upon earth.[7]

Soon afterwards we read the first-hand account of the Centurion's slave being healed by the power of Jesus.

> *After a little I opened my eyes; a light shone around me, so brilliant that I had to turn from it again, and only gradually become accustomed to its brightness. Then I saw that it flowed out from One Person, in whom it centered. O, what glory surrounded Him! And yet His greatest glory seemed to me to lie in that look of deep pity and of intense love with which He regarded me. I was now also aware that it was His hand which arrested my fall. His arm still supported me, as He knelt by my side, gazing with unspeakable compassion into my face. I could not speak, but I looked up to Him in mute appeal for help; I felt as if with Him rested my last, my only hope of safety. As I looked, it seemed to flow like balm into my bruised, wounded body. The pain ceased, the weariness left me. Then I felt as if racking torment were no longer creeping down my brain and along my limbs; as if the dark shadow were moving away from over me. I lifted my hand to Him who still supported me against His heart. He pointed me upwards; mine eyes followed. Can I ever forget it? It was as if a luminous track stretched from the spot where we were into heaven itself. The clouds were cleft, all was so near. There stood a great white throne, surrounded by what seemed a rainbow; harpers were harping so sweetly, white robed messengers were coming and going, and all around stood a countless multitude. Yet all this, though so glorious, inspired me with joy rather than with awe; for He that had rescued and still supported me, now pressed me closer to His heart, and held me up, as it were, by His strength. I felt so calm and happy, I wished to be always there. What length of time passed while I was in this state I have never accurately ascertained; they who watched beside me, however, narrowly observed me. They say that all at once my face and hands seemed bathed in perspiration. As they bent over, imagining that the last conflict had come, they noticed that a heavenly light had come across me. It was like a sunbeam creeping in that streamed around – a golden light rested upon my face. They thought that I saw visions of the blessed, and expected every moment*

---

7. July 1, 1869

> to see me draw my last breath; but it was otherwise – my colour was heightening, the flush of health was returning; my features ceased to be right, my limbs to be stiff and cramped. While they wondered at this great change, the sunbeam that had rested upon me faded from sight. Gentle deep sleep, like that of a child, held me.[8]

The narrative continues with bold descriptions of Jerusalem during Passover week and the priestly functions in the temple. As Marcos was celebrating the Passover the ancient traditions raised more questions in his mind.

> One thing has struck me as very remarkable. All the prophecies of the Messiah are full of the hope of the Ingathering of the Gentiles; yet we are never told that they will be circumcised. Thus they will not be qualified to take part in our Paschal services, as indeed what is purely national could scarcely apply to them. What then? Will the Passover be abolished? This cannot be. Or shall it be so enlarged, both in meaning and in form, as somehow to become a feast to the Gentiles as well as for Israel?[9]

The story continues with subplots, further accounts of miracles from the man from Nazareth, and grand expectations. But sadly, the remaining chapters of this novel do not exist. Whether he stopped writing or the chapters appear elsewhere, they are not part of the Scattered Nation collection.

---

8. January 1, 1870, p. 5
9. January 1, 1870, p. 37

Appendix C

The Athenaeum

THE FOLLOWING BOOKS WERE reviewed by Alfred Edersheim in the publication, The Athenaeum, between the years 1856 and 1861. The reviews vary in length from just a few sentences to one or two pages. The various topics give insight into the broad range of his expertise.

August 9, 1856, *Jerusalem and Tiberius; Sora and Cordova: A Survey of the Religious and Scholastic Learning of the Jews,* by Dr. J.W. Ethridge

December 13, 1856, *An Introduction of the Critical Study and Knowledge of the Hebrew Scriptures,* by Rev. Thomas Hartwell Horne etc

January 27, 1857, *The English Harmony of the Four Gospels,* by Dr. Allen

Travels of Rabbi Petachia of Ratisbon, by Dr. A. Benisch

January 31, 1857, *A Narrative of Dan Angel Herreros de Mora,* by Rev. W.H. Rule

March 14, 1857, *The History and Life of the Rev. Dr. John Tauler of Strasbourg,* by Susanna Winkworth

June 6, 1857, *Travels and Researches in Chaldea and Susiana,* by William Kenneth Loftus

December 5, 1857, *Life in Israel; or Portraitures of Hebrew Character,* by Maria Richards

Appendix C

December 19, 1857, *Jewish Literature from the Eighth to the Eighteenth Century*, by M. Steinschneider

March 20, 1858, *The Historical Connection of the Old and New Testaments*, by Humphrey Prideaux

March 22, 1858, *Essays on Various Subjects, Philological, Philosophical, Ethnological and Archaeological*, by John Williams

July 17, 1858, *The Book of Job, translated from the Hebrew on the basis of the Authorized Version*, by Rev. C.P. Carey

July 24, 1858, *A Historical and Critical Commentary on the Old Testament*, by M.M. Kalisch

October 9, 1858, *A Historical-Critical Introduction to the canonical Books of the New Testament*, by William M. L. De Watt

February 26, 1859, *City of the Great King; or, Jerusalem as it was, as it is, and as it is to be*, by J. T. Barclay

March 19, 1859, *History of the Knights of Malta*, by Major Whitworth Porter

April 2, 1859, *The Book of Job: the Common English Version, the Hebrew Text*, and the revised Version, by T.J. Conant

April 9, 1859, *A Handbook for Travelers in Syria and Palestine*, by Dr. Murray

May 14, 1859, *To Jerusalem!*, by Ludwig Aug. Frankl

July 2, 1859, *History of the Christian Church, from the Thirteenth Century to the Present Day*, by Rev. Alfred Lyell etc

September 17, 1859, *The English Bible: According to the Authorized Version, newly divided into paragraphs and Sections etc.*, by Dr. Allan

The Athenaeum

November 5, 1859, *The Land and the Book*, by W.W. Thomson

March 31, 1860, *Ishmael, or, a Natural History of Islamism, and its Relation to Christianity*, by Dr. I. Muehleisen Arnold

June 16, 1860, *Inquiry into the Original Language of St. Matthew's Gospel*, by Rev. Alexander Roberts

July 7, 1860, *A Dictionary of the Bible, Comprising its Antiquities, Biographies, geography and Natural History*, edited by William Smith

November 17, 1860, *The Annotated Paragraph Bible*, by the Religious Tract Society

February 2, 1861, *The History of the Creation and the Patriarchs*, by Chapman

July 20, 1861, *The Church History of Scotland*, by Rev. John Cunningham

Appendix D

Eulogy from a Fellow Oxford Professor

Dr. William Sanday was professor of exegesis at Exeter College, Oxford. On May 12th of 1889 he delivered a sermon in their chapel which was called *The Example of a Christian Scholar, with Some Remarks on the State of Learning in Oxford*. It is mostly about Edersheim, who had passed away several weeks earlier. Below are the passages from the sermon which specifically speak of him.

∽

On the last Saturday of last Term there went to his rest an adopted member of the college who yet loved and was proud of it as if it had been his own. Many who are here will remember a striking-looking figure which was often to be seen at our Sunday Services, especially at the mid-day Communion before the change in the hour. A mind naturally academic took an especial pleasure in these services, just as others may as naturally prefer those of the parish churches which remind them of their homes. For the last two terms the figure of which I speak was missing from its place. A summer of ill-health, combated in vain, had made it necessary to seek a milder clime [sic] and to give some repose to an incessantly working brain. For a long time all seemed to be going well. Only good news traveled northwards. We heard of recovered health and spirits. Work was resumed. The Grinfield Lectures, which were to be given in the present term, were prepared. Many other literary plans were being laid. Above all the reading, wide and deep, was being prosecuted which was to serve as the foundation for the volumes which were to continue a great work, auspiciously begun, the crowning moment of a studious life.

... Our friend who came to settle among us understood what learning was. He was himself a learned man in the true sense of the word. Let any one turn the pages of his great work devoted to a great subject, or even lesser products of his pen like the articles in the *Dictionary of Christian Biography*, or the *Commentary on Ecclesiasticus*, and he will feel at once that he is in the presence of a mind that has not its knowledge from compendia, but has really steeped and saturated itself with the subject. A mind of any individuality naturally takes a line of its own; and here this line was marked by descent and antecedents. The Jews who have embraced Christianity have been among the most learned of its exponents. They bring with them a native aptitude for the study of the conditions under which Christianity arose. And our friend had, I believe, in this respect hardly an equal. Look at the mass of details with which [the *Life and Times of Jesus the Messiah*] are crowded, observe the precision and sureness of statement, and you will recognise the hand of a master. I admit that this is on a popular line, that other sides of the book were addressed to a popular audience, and that it had its deficiencies. The author himself was fully aware of these deficiencies. He had hoped if he had been spared to supply them later. To some extent at least perhaps they might have been supplied. To what extent must be matter of speculation, and not of very important speculation. . . . For death cut short a career that had not begun to decline, but had reached the culmination and full maturity of its powers.

. . . Here was one who was "in diligence not slothful; fervent in spirit," but in all that he did and in the deepest foundation of his nature "serving the Lord." He appreciated learning; he did not appreciate playing at learning; perhaps he hardly did full justice to the value of our system as a training-ground for better things. He was never weary of holding up high ideals to his friends; he would not let them decline from these; and he was quite capable of being caustic upon anything that he thought pretentious and hollow. I know on the other hand what rejoicing he greeted the signs that he saw of earnest purpose and determination in younger men. There are some whom I would bid remember as a stimulus to exertion that – 'He watches from his grave." – But though he thus appreciated it by every means in his power, though he thoroughly understood and valued it for its own sake, in himself it was consecrated to yet higher ends.

The gravest complaint that was brought against his writings was that they showed a want of criticism. The complaint had its truth. But this was not, as I have said elsewhere, from indifference to criticism. It was rather that criticism was postponed. The order he preferred was exposition first, criticism afterwards. Not perhaps a strictly logical order, or an order

Appendix D

which it would be well for everyone to follow, but one which has much to be said for its certain cases. You cannot criticize properly until you know; and the process of knowing may well take a life-time. Our friend was cautious and circumspect by nature. He felt his way before he took his step, and he was fearful of touching and profaning the ark of the Lord.

It was the same reason, or the same kind of reason, which caused so much of his work to be taken up with apologetics. He wished to defend the inheritance which has come down to us from the past from what he thought rude assaults. Having previously in his own life undergone two great mental changes – the first out of strong conviction, at the cost of much personal cost and privation, the second by a slow growth of logical necessity from his lively apprehension of the historical side of our faith – and having through these changes preserved unimpaired the bases of his religion, he was loth [sic] to admit by which it seemed possible that they might be shaken. I will not say that in this attitude of mind he may not have defended positions which may prove to be tenable. I will not say that to some this caution might not wear an appearance of timidity. It was certainly at the opposite pole of that rashness which "Steps in where angels fear to tread." He knew the responsibility of belief. And though he would give a calm and patient hearing to those who spoke in opposition to his own views but really knowing what they said, he was not very tolerant of the sciolism [sic] which on the strength of a mere smattering of knowledge seeks to destroy what it cannot rebuild. He may not always have been right. We are fallible mortals, and we may any of us choose a wrong point to give up or maintain. But we may be sure at least of this, that the great readjustment which is going on will have to be worked out in the market place but in the study, not in novels or magazines but by a long collection and sifting of data, and by much laborious as well as chastened thought.

Those who are engaged in this process may well take encouragement from the example that is set before them. As they look back upon the career that is past they may well compose their minds, and casting away unchristian regrets they may join in that calm and beautiful prayer: "We also bless Thy Holy Name for all Thy servants departed this life in Thy faith and fear; beseeching Thee to give us grace so to follow their good examples, that with them we may be partakers of Thy heavenly Kingdom: Grant this, O Father, for Jesus Christ's sake, our only Mediator and Advocate. Amen."

www.ingramcontent.com/pod-product-compliance
Lightning Source LLC
Chambersburg PA
CBHW062036220426
43662CB00010B/1527